PROFESSIONALS AND THEIR WORK IN THE FAMILY DIVORCE COURT

PROFESSIONALS AND THEIR WORK IN THE FAMILY DIVORCE COURT

By

EDWARD GUMZ, PH.D.

The University of Wisconsin, Oshkosh

CHARLES C THOMAS • PUBLISHER

Springfield • Illinois • U.S.A.

Published and Distributed Throughout the World by

CHARLES C THOMAS • PUBLISHER
2600 South First Street
Springfield, Illinois 62794-9265

ISBN 0-398-05304-9

Library of Congress Catalog Card Number: 86-23074

With THOMAS BOOKS *careful attention is given to all details of manufacturing and design. It is the Publisher's desire to present books that are satisfactory as to their physical qualities and artistic possibilities and appropriate for their particular use.* THOMAS BOOKS *will be true to those laws of quality that assure a good name and good will.*

Printed in the United States of America
Q-R-3

Library of Congress Cataloging in Publication Data

Gumz, Edward.
Professionals and their work in the family divorce court.

Bibliography: p.
Includes index.
1. Domestic relations courts--United States.
2. Family counselors--United States. I. Title.
KF505.5.G86 1987 346.7301'0269 86-23074
ISBN 0-398-05304-9 347.306150269

For . . .
Marie, Liz, Andy and Jon

PREFACE

A PROBLEM endemic to all organizations, in fact to social life itself, is the matter of how to explain discrepancies or gaps between what is and what is supposed to be, between the actual and the ideal. The formal/rational model of organizations tends to focus on organizational efforts to achieve rationality in terms of an overall design and mission. When discrepancies occur, it is due to the organization not achieving its goals. Discrepancies are dealt with by setting limits on individual actions and acts by a controlling group.

Another, divergent framework which deals with the issue of organizational rationality is that of the institutional school of organizations. From this point of view each organization is seen as having a history which is of relevance in terms of shaping current organizational functioning. An organization consists of more than its formal statements; rather its essence is found in uncovering the realities of social systems and in examining deviations within the organization. From an institutional viewpoint organizational discrepancies are dealt with by the competitive strivings of internal groups and by the process of institutionalization in which the organization adapts to the values of the external society (Perrow, 1979: 186).

Recently a specific type of human service organization has received considerable attention. Hasenfeld (1972), Prottas (1979), and Lipsky (1980) have put forth the concept of people-processing organizations or street-level bureaucracies. The primary function of these organizations is not to directly change the behavior of persons, but rather to process them and confer public statuses on them. They defy any precise organizational analysis because their goals are often unclear, their resources to do assigned work in short supply, and their leadership unsure about what service providers actually do. Thus, these organizations are unable to deal with discrepancies — to bring into line what really happens in the organization with the organization's formal goals. Perhaps as a result of this, street-level bureaucrats or professionals* in these organizations possess substantial discretion to make decisions which frequently significantly affect the life course of people seen.

In order to comprehend the work of these professionals in their organizational work environment, what they do must be studied at close range through a series of observations and interviews. For this task the works of Berger and Luckmann (1966) and Garfinkel (1967) on how participants go about making sense of their work in organizations where the social order is tenuous and continually emergent are of special relevance.

Neither the formal/organizational model nor the institutional model by itself can adequately explain the work of a street-level bureaucracy. Therefore, references to both models in elucidating the work of a particular type of street-level bureaucracy will be made.

In what follows I briefly describe this study, the importance of the setting where the research takes place, and present an overview of chapter contents.

The research results reported here are based on a field study of a family court in a large, midwestern urban community. As has been alluded to earlier, a problem common to organizational life is the maintenance of order. The formal/rational model of organizations focuses on organizational efforts to achieve rationality in terms of an organization's historical mission. The institutional school focuses on how discrepancies are dealt with by strivings among organizational groups. However, while this is occurring, the goals of the organization are also being shaped by its institutional environment. While this is taking place, professionals need to make sense out of their work on a daily basis, and to do this, make use of aligning actions or "accounts." Sometimes these practices merge with broad organizational goals, at other times not. The problem is to explain this continual tension between the historical aim for overall design on the one hand, and particular ("street-level") organizational articulations, on the other. In addition to examining practices of professionals and the formal organization's structure, the institutional environment which shapes both the organization and professional work life needs to be understood.

The Study and the Site

The family court can be viewed as a unique type of human service organization. It represents an effort to combine legal and therapeutic

*In this study the terms street-level bureaucrats and professionals will be used interchangeably.

frames of reference to deal with a wide range of domestic relations matters as separation, visitation, and custody. The first family court was founded in the United States in New York City in 1910 thus making it a relatively recent phenomenon.

Sociologists have demonstrated a long-standing interest in studying relationships between the law and social processes. In spite of this, sociological interest in the courts seems to be uneven. Criminal courts have received substantial attention so that some highly specific areas such as plea bargaining have been written about fairly extensively (Heumann, 1975; Cressey, 1977; Littrell, 1979).

Of equal, perhaps even greater interest to sociologists than the criminal court has been the study of the juvenile court. Originally considered to be an "experiment" aimed at dealing with delinquency, the juvenile court was created in the United States in 1899. It has been studied from the vantage point of social control (Platt, 1969) and of social change (Ryerson, 1976). The latest sociological monograph on the work of the juvenile court is that of Fabricant (1983) who examined the current functioning of the juvenile court system in New York City.

While both criminal and juvenile courts have received considerable attention from sociologists, the family court has not. A review of the sociological literature from 1964-1985 as reported in *Sociological Abstracts* indicates that no studies have been done regarding the functioning of the family court in general and more specifically the role of professionals in service provision. The reasons for this are unclear, but some speculations can be made. The matters with which the family court deals are of a civil and domestic, not criminal, nature. Often these matters are more mundane and less dramatic for study than those dealt with in criminal courts. In addition, while the sociology of the family is a well-established subspecialty of the field, it has paid primary attention to the family as an institution and has not shown substantial interest in the interface between the family and other institutions. (For a recent, notable exception, see Gubrium, 1983.)

Although sociologists have not shown an interest in analyzing the functioning of the family court and the role of service providers within it, it is a topic of relevance. Both the popular and professional literature make reference to family change as expressed in divorce (Wallerstein and Kelly, 1980), child support (Cassetty, 1978), and nontraditional custody arrangements (Roman and Haddad, 1978). Although statistics on divorce rates are bandied about rather casually, what is of importance here is that divorce and the attendent problems of child custody and support have become thorny legal and sociological issues (*Marquette Law Review*, "Special Issues on Family Law", 1983). Professionals in the court—be they judges, commissioners, or social workers—make crucial decisions which influence an individual's family relationships for years. A striking example is that in a custody battle a judge can decide with which parent a child will live, thus dramatically shaping the life course of that child. Hopefully this study will illuminate the work of the family court and how professionals there go about doing their work and make decisions.

Organization

In Chapter One I present how I became interested in the work of the family court. This is followed by a more formal presentation of the methodology for the study. This is a field study in which I made use of several techniques to gather data. Historical material was examined to understand the origins of the court both nationally and locally. Observations and extensive, focused interviews with the professionals at the court—judges, commissioners, and social workers—were used to gather data about the contemporary court. A typology of accounts was constructed and the accounts of service providers at the court were compared and contrasted.

The history of the court both nationally and locally is reviewed in Chapter Two. Social forces which gave rise to the court are examined along with efforts to bring about organizational rationality or wholeness. At the local level, documentary materials and interviews of persons who have been instrumental in shaping the court's history were used. The family court as a legal entity is also examined and how its sociolegal work is shaped by a changing institutional environment.

The basic problem with which this study contends is presented and elaborated on in Chapter Three. Briefly, it is how discrepancies or gaps between what is and what is supposed to be are dealt with in an organization so that rationality or the organizing of human activity around purpose can be maintained. The formal/rational and institutional frameworks discussed earlier in the Preface are elaborated. Street-level bureaucracy is seen as a particular organizational form brought about by a lack of clarity in organizational goals, which is in turn fostered by a rapidly changing institutional environment. With the organization in an anomic state, the work of the individual, autonomous professional takes on increased importance as the organizational work role is socially constructed bereft of any strong organizational leadership and assistance.

In discussing the work of professionals the term "account" is of crucial importance in this study and while it will be discussed in great detail in Chapter Three some clarification of the term is in order at this point. In this study, the term "account" is used in its sociological sense, meaning statements made to explain unanticipated actions (Scott and Lyman, 1968). Accounts in the form of statements as explanations, excuses, or justifications are a crucial element in the social order since they prevent conflict from breaking out by verbally bridging the gap between action and expectation. Accounts are in essence aligning actions and key elements in the creation of rationality. By comparing and contrasting accounts of professionals in the court a view of how work is done is obtained.

Chapters Four, Five, and Six provide an examination of how service providers within the court go about doing their work. On the basis of observations and interviews, judges, social workers, and commissioners interpretations of their work is presented using the typology of accounts. The interpretations of what they do are compared and contrasted.

In the Conclusion, some tentative answers to the presenting problem are discussed along with observations of people-processing organizations in general. Some final observations regarding the methodology for the study are made with suggestions for further research. Finally, modest proposals for change in the court under study are presented.

ACKNOWLEDGMENTS

I WOULD LIKE to thank all of the individuals who work in the family court which I studied. They unselfishly gave of their time to share with me their views of their work, with all its frustrations and possibilities. In particular, I wish to thank the judges, commissioners, and social workers of the court who talked with me and permitted me to observe them in their professional work. Certainly without their helpfulness, this study could never have been done.

My former teachers, Ann Lennarson Greer, Scott Greer, and Jaber Gubrium, all outstanding sociologists, gave me a good share of their intellectual curiosity which led me to the topic of professional work in the family court. I heartily thank them. I also wish to thank Attorneys Harry Theuerkauf and William Whitten, Jr., longtime friends with whom I could discuss the court as a legal entity.

Finally, I wish to thank my wife, Marie, without whose love and ongoing support this study would not have been completed. Thanks to my children—Jonathan, Andrew, and Elizabeth. Their question, "Dad, when are you going to be finished?" was no doubt an important factor in the completion of the project.

CONTENTS

PROFESSIONALS AND THEIR WORK IN THE FAMILY DIVORCE COURT

CHAPTER ONE

METHODOLOGY: DOING THE STUDY

Initial Interest

I HAVE HAD a long-standing interest in and concern for the functioning of families in my career as a social worker. In addition, my years in social work have been spent working in organizations where human services are delivered within a bureaucratic context and, as a result, I have become aware of the organizational supports and constraints which shape the role of the human service provider.

My interest in the area of the family and organizational influences on service delivery was intensified, when in early 1982, I became involved in a counseling situation with a family where the twelve-year-old son was part of a joint custody arrangement. Aside from the clinical matters inherent in such a situation, this case touched on post-divorce arrangements for children and also raised questions regarding how legal and social work professionals reach decisions regarding joint custody phenomena.

In reviewing the literature on these subjects regarding the interface between organizations and the family, I found that little had been written. However, one notable work is that of sociologist Paul Tappan, entitled *Delinquent Girls in Court,* a book which examined the work of the juvenile court in New York City in 1957. Of particular interest was Tappan's detailed analysis of how judges and probation officers disposed of cases, using discretion to decide which girls were to be placed on probation and which sent to juvenile homes. Tappan details the processes whereby professionals in the court reached these decisions. While being an excellent monograph on the work of the juvenile court, it also describes the practice of law and social work within an organizational setting. Tappan's work aroused my interest in exploring the work of professionals in the family court, how they go about doing their work, and what impact the decisions which they make have upon the family.

In looking for works about the family court *per se,* I was surprised to discover only a few. One was an article by L. B. Day (1928) who discussed the growth of the early family court nationally. However, there were no book-length descriptions of the court. I decided to make some contacts at the family court in Milwaukee to hopefully learn more about it first-hand. Assuming that the warmest response to my inquiries about the court might come from a fellow social worker, I contacted a senior social worker at the court, Robert Frances. "Bob," as he is called, was eager to talk with me not only about joint custody, but also about the work of the court in general and the functioning of legal professionals and social workers within it. Bob turned out to be a most helpful informant during the course of the study. His insights into the functioning of the court, his comments about court personnel (which I was careful to check out) and his considerateness, as finding an office for me which I could use during the study for making field notes and just thinking, characterized his helpfulness. In ways such as these, he can be compared with Doc who was helpful to Whyte (1955) in his work, *Street-Corner Society.* After I first met Bob, he introduced me to the Chief Family Court Commissioner who was a proponent of joint custody. I talked with him and also the Deputy Court Commissioner. Not only was my interest in the court further stimulated by conversations with these persons, but observing the waiting area to the commissioners' hearing rooms made an impression on me. The court seemed to be bewildering, fast-paced, and not staid—all descriptions quite contrary to my previously held view of the courts as being staid, slow and inert. This observation spurred me on to discover how professionals went about doing their work in this kind of atmosphere.

Refining the Topic

My interest in the court continued so I decided to do some first hand observations of how professionals went about doing their work in the family court. I observed the group sessions for reconciliation conducted by the social workers, interviewed six social workers, and interviewed and observed in the hearing rooms of two commissioners. The family court as a formal organization remained somewhat of a riddle to me, but a review of the literature regarding human service organizations was helpful. Especially useful was Hasenfeld's (1972) work on people-processing organizations, Prottas' (1979) work on people processors, and Lipsky's (1980) work on street-level bureaucracy.

In selecting the family court as a topic I soon realized that the focus needed to be narrowed. Because of my personal and academic interest in the work of human service providers, organizational factors in their work, and the demands of the formal organization upon them, I decided to look closely at their work and how they made sense of it. Because I had observed at the family court previously, I realized that diverse and rich data was there, and the best way to understand it was by means of a field study based on observations and interviews. Becker (1969: 331) indicated that participant observation is the method of choice when the sociologist is interested in understanding a particular organization rather than demonstrating relations between abstractly defined variables. This type of research has theoretical relevance when not enough is known about the organization *a priori* to identify specific problems. Hypotheses are generated in the course of the research.

While I was thinking about the methodology for the study, I also was concerned about how time constraints would limit the scope and depth of the study. Based on my earlier observations at the court, I had learned that schedules there were quite unpredictable—hearings could be prolonged, move quickly, or be cancelled. On the basis of this, I believed that it was necessary to spend blocks of time—whole days and half days—to obtain the necessary data but also to make it easier to get at in-depth material. I was able to arrange for a half-time leave of absence from my job enabling me to spend about four months, from September to December, 1984, averaging about twenty hours per week in this field study of the court.

While I was making these arrangements, I also checked with Bob at the court to determine how cooperative the chief judge at the court would be in permitting such research at the court. Bob seemed to feel that there would be no problems, and I felt reassured. However, I suggested a meeting with the chief judge, chief commissioner, and Bob to discuss the proposed research and gain their consent. The meeting was scheduled, but prior to the meeting I provided a one page description of the proposed study for the persons at the meeting. I also assured them that references would be handled in a confidential manner. The meeting went well, there were no objections to doing the study at the court, and I was elated. Shortly after the meeting the chief judge circulated a memorandum to court personnel introducing me and asking for their cooperation in the study. One matter from the meeting is worth an additional comment. In the description of the study I indicated that the court "dealt with matters of family disorganization." There was some opposition to this phrase in the meeting; it was felt that the court helps families "reorganize," to deal with family break-up. I did not realize it at the time, but this was a significant statement about the perceived role and function of the court. As a result, I was led to question, "If the court assists in family re-organization, how do different professionals go about doing this?"

When it became time to write up the findings of this research, I debated to what extent it was necessary to disguise the site of the research; I concluded that this was not essential for the protection of human subjects. In fact, doing this would be extremely difficult because of newspaper articles and judges' references to the Milwaukee family court in several periodicals which were cited.

In reporting my observations and interviews in the contemporary court, I used pseudonyms to maintain the anonymity of the respondents. It is interesting to note that in no interview did the respondent raise the issue of confidentiality. Either it was not an issue of importance or the respondent trusted me to handle the material in a confidential manner. In reporting interviews with persons active in the court in the past actual names were used since important newspaper and journal references cited made any use of pseudonyms impossible.

Rainwater and Pittman (1967) deal with the ethical issues in fieldwork, particularly the problem of confidentiality. While providing anonymity in all respects in any field study is extremely difficult, they suggest that the sociologist has an ethical duty to protect the rights of his subjects while also elucidating the social systems of which these persons are a part.

Starting in Earnest

I was ready to begin. As I entered the courthouse one Monday morning in September, I felt eager to get started yet also uneasy and anxious as to just how to begin. It was helpful during the early phase of fieldwork to have a contact person at the court like Bob with whom I could talk about the court as a whole and obtain background information. As I learned more about the court and developed greater confidence in my ability to explore the court on my own, I spent less time with Bob. I decided that initially I would observe and interview the social workers. I already knew them from previous observations at the court and knew that they would be receptive to talking with me. This proved to be the case. While I was doing this I believed that it was important to show

how the court developed and how some of its functions have changed over time. Therefore a history of the court needed to be done. I thought it would be necessary to review important memoranda, notes from key meetings, etc. I found in talking with court personnel that such documents, if available at all, were scattered around in different offices. An administrative assistant, Beatrice Allen, was very helpful in locating for me some documents about the history of the family court commissioners in the county.

It was also suggested that I contact two former chief family court judges, now retired, who had considerable knowledge about the court. I decided to do this and interviewed both. In addition, I spent time in the courthouse law library. This is open to all Milwaukee County residents but is used primarily by practicing attorneys for legal research. The library has an extensive collection of legal periodicals and some books. I perused the journals on family law and found no articles which specifically dealt with the socio-legal aspects of family law, as dealt with in an organizational setting. However, while at the library I discovered that newspaper clippings of the work of specific courts in the county are on file in the library. For example, there is a collection of articles on the family court in Milwaukee County from both of Milwaukee's major newspapers, *The Milwaukee Journal* and *Milwaukee Sentinel,* culled by courthouse librarians. I decided to use these reports for a history of the court; these reports provided a continuing record of the court from the 1950's to the present. In addition, interviews with two retired Chief Family Court Judges (active in the court during the 1960's and 1970's) mentioned earlier served to produce more evidence regarding significant past events in the court.

Interviews and Observations

While documents about the court and interviews with judges were the basis for the history of the court, interviews and observations were used in the study of the contemporary court. Becker (1969: 28-32) examined interviewing techniques in relation to participant observation. He noted that observation provides a rich experiential context which sensitizes the researcher to incongruous or unexplained facts. I might add that these incongruities can be explored within the interview. This was my experience in observing in courtrooms and hearing rooms, noting unexplained facts and then following this up in subsequent interviews.

Denzin (1978: 129) also commented on the relationship between interviewing and observation noting that a good interviewer is by necessity also a participant observer. The interviewer participates in the life experiences of the respondent while observing the individual's report of himself or herself during the interview. Denzin believes that the good interviewer attempts to become a part of the social worlds of experience which are being studied.

Interviews were a crucial part of this study for it was from them that data about how professionals view their work at the court was obtained. All judges, commissioners, and social workers were interviewed except for one commissioner who persistently refused, indicating that the chief commissioner could answer my questions. I learned that this commissioner had problems at one time in talking with a newspaper reporter. He was misquoted, I believe, and as a result did not cooperate when I indicated I wanted to talk with him. In addition to interviewing professionals at the court in their work setting, I also talked with clerical, administrative personnel, court clerks, and bailiffs.

Prior to my interviewing the professional personnel at the court, I formulated a list of questions which I believed would be helpful in eliciting responses regarding how professionals viewed their work at the court. However, the particular phrasing of questions and their order were redefined to fit the characteristics of each respondent. For example, questions took into consideration the fact that social workers, judges, and commissioners receive different professional training and hence their understanding of such things as intra-familial factors may vary. The form of interview used most closely approximated what has been called the focused interview. (Merton and Kendall, 1946: 541-52). All professionals at the court except for the one commissioner mentioned earlier were interviewed at least once with more than half being interviewed two or three times. Most respondents were interviewed in their work settings, but interview-conversations with several persons were also held in the courthouse coffee shop.

The art of interviewing in the social sciences has been written about extensively and I attempted to incorporate some of the material into my interviewing. Lofland (1971: 100) advocated a personal interviewing style which he described as follows: "be non-threatening, be supportive, be interested." Dean, Eichorn, and Dean (Dean et al, 1967: 302) talked about the need for the interviewer to be an analytic listener who appraises the meaning of emerging data for his problem and uses the resulting insights to phrase questions that will elucidate the implications of the data. Mauksch's statement was succinct. "Follow the professional's trail of personal experience in the court." (Personal conversation with Professor Hans Mauksch, University of Wisconsin-Milwaukee, Department of Sociology, September 19, 1984).

In addition to the task of obtaining usable data from interviews, a decision needed to be made as to how this material was to be recorded. I decided against the use of a tape recorder since it would reduce the spontaneity of interviewees. Also, I did not have the resources available for the transcription of interviews. My remaining choices were to take notes on the interview as it progressed and write a fuller report later or to take notes on the interview after it concluded and then write it up. I decided that since interviewees' views of their work at the court was an essential element of the study, I should record these descriptions verbatim. I improved my skill in doing this but also realized that I perhaps was not able to follow up productive leads. While I attempted to record verbatim interviewees' descriptions of their work, I also jotted down key words or phrases for later follow-up, perhaps in another interview. After each interview I usually returned to my office, recorded some overall impressions, tried to fill in gaps in the interview, and noted comments which needed follow-up. Recording observations in waiting areas of the court and processing of cases in courtrooms or hearing rooms was easier than recording interviews. Of course, interchanges between judges and litigants were difficult to record; a disadvantage here is that I could not ask for clarification about a certain point as could be done in an interview.

Organizing the Data

As I studied historical documents about the court, observed there, and interviewed participants, the volume of data grew continually and about half way through my period of observation at the court I tried to impose meaningful order on this large amount of data. I continued to read about theories of organization, street-level bureaucracy, and people-processing organizations. Gaps between what transpires at a formal level of an organization and what takes place on a micro level in service encounters within the organization were evident from my observations. This led me to explore the works of Garfinkel (1967), Sudnow (1965), and Emerson (1977) who have researched how people go about making sense out of their social world by offering justifications, explanations, and excuses for a wide range of social acts. The approaches of the authors just cited touch on the matter of how people come to know social reality. An influential book for me in this area was Berger and Luckmann's (1966) *The Social Construction of Reality* which deals with how micro and macro levels of social reality are created and maintained; in essence this work is a treatise on the sociology of knowledge.

Up until this point in my interviews with and observations of bureaucrats at the court, I had noticed that the formal organization offered few guidelines to professionals to do their work, to dispose of cases—in a sense, to be good organizational actors. But judges, commissioners, and social workers went about doing their work—processing people among other things—and in doing this developed a rationality to make sense out of what they did. In this work, the professionals assumed the role of street-level bureaucrats. They acted quite autonomously, they all worked for an organization which had few or no explicit goals, and resources to do their work were chronically inadequate (Lipsky: 1980).

While Weber viewed bureaucracy as a unitary phenomenon, Lipsky looked at the underside of bureaucracy and began to examine the processes whereby bureaucrats in human service settings went about fulfilling their roles. However, Lipsky did not examine differences and similarities among street-level bureaucrats in organizational settings. He assumed that there are basically two levels of organizational rationality—one, that of the formal organization, and the other, that of street-level bureaucrats. In my observations and interviews at the court I seemed to be finding several levels of rationality—that of the formal organization, but also differing rationalities of different professions—judges, commissioners, and social workers. In order to examine these rationalities it was necessary to develop an organizing framework within which to compare and contrast bureaucrats' views of their work.

I began to explore the rather murky literature regarding how actors deal with social structure. A review of this literature can be found in Chapter Three (page 34 ff.) of this study. I decided to use Scott and Lyman's (1968) concept of accounts (actors' explanations of their actions) as a means of determining the experience and maintenance of social structure within the court.

Based on my interviews and observations at the court I was led to believe that professionals use a variety of accounts to go about achieving rationality in their work. In order to test this proposition I decided to construct a typology of accounts which could be used as a basis for comparison of empirical cases. Data gathered up until this point seemed to indicate that accounts centered on people, organizational elements, and ideologies or belief-systems. Each of these items seemed to have both internal and external dimensions so that six types of accounts could be used to compare and contrast bureaucrats' views of their work (See Chapter Three, p. 44).

For example, internal-personal accounts refer to clients or litigants who are processed by professionals in their official organizational roles. External-personal accounts deal with persons outside the court who have an important role in facilitating the work of the bureaucrat—lawyers, for example. Internal-organizational factors such as other professionals in the organization and their roles serve as another basis for accounts. External-organizational factors such as another organization, the legislature, for example, serve a role in the work of the court professional. External-ideological accounts deal with belief systems of the broader society and how these shape the work of service providers in the court.

With this kind of organizing framework, I continued to gather data but also began to do some coding on data already collected. I studied interviews and began to code the accounts using the typology; I realized quickly that in doing this I was not using precise, positivist procedures. Rather I was in the early stages of developing an interpretive understanding of the data. Wax (1967: 326) indicates that such an understanding requires grasping "the vast background of shared meanings" through which the social world is organized into socially recognized categories. The pace of the research quickened notably as I found myself doing many things—gathering data, coding, and analysis. I began to do some preliminary writing—looking at the internal-personal accounts of judges and comparing these with the social workers' accounts. By doing this I tested the adequacy of the typology but also recognized gaps where I needed to obtain more data. Returning for more data was easier than initial data collection because I knew what I was looking for. For example, in examining the work of the commissioners I discovered that they view initial hearings as an important part of their role. I examined this and found that their role is usually different in first hearings than other hearings. However, I needed to obtain more evidence to confirm this proposition, so I focused on first hearings by observing and interviewing commissioners about them. Finally, I was satisfied that I had gathered enough evidence to make a definitive statement about commissioners' roles in initial hearings.

Analysis

As the research proceeded, I began to be tempted to spend more time on analysis of the data. Yet I knew because of time considerations, I could not do this since more interviews and observations had to be made. So I gathered more data indicating to persons that I was finishing up and thanked them for their cooperation. After the formal part of the research was completed, I stopped at the court several times to make some observations, to fill in data-gaps, and simply to talk with persons at the court. Typical questions asked of me were, "How is it [the research] coming?" "When are you going to finish it?" "Can we read it?"

As I completed the fieldwork at the court, I continued to organize the data, analyze it, and think about ways of presenting it. I learned that presenting data gathered from the field is a difficult task. Lofland (1971: 128-29) indicates that penetrating and useful qualitative analysis strikes a balance between theoretical concepts on the one hand and descriptions of the setting on the other. On the one side there is the error of analytic excess in which one becomes so engrossed in the logic of abstract analysis that one does not report much of the concrete reality to which the categories refer. On the other side there is the error of descriptive excess. This is the practice of becoming so engrossed in presenting concrete details that one loses any connection with analytic categories that illumine these concrete details. Lofland calls for balanced reporting—namely analytic description—and this is what I aimed for. I found this difficult; for example, based on my experiences in social work, I found it easy to be analytic when discussing the social work role. However, in discussing the work of the commissioners, the impact of the physical setting upon their work may have led to some descriptive excess in reporting. Overall, a major task of reporting was to explain how various bureaucrats viewed their work and also to compare and contrast the rationalities of the three professions working within the court. The validity of several theoretical frameworks for understanding service provision was examined in light of the data about the court.

Cicourel (1964: 3) observes that in fieldwork "the observer is part of the field of action." One way to interpret this statement is that fieldwork is experiential for the researcher. I found myself empathizing with the clients who were seen in the court. For many it meant that sorrowful collapse of the dream of a stable family life; for a few it meant welcome relief that a bad situation had ended and hope for a better future. But these concerns led to other questions about the court such as, "How much bureaucratic discretion is justifiable?" "How can an organization as the family court with no stated goals be of help to individuals in distress?" "Finally, does the court not only process individuals but also families and how might changes be introduced into this procedure?" These are some of the questions which on the basis of my research at the court I was led to ask. It is these issues which I discuss in the final chapter and which can serve as an impetus for further research.

CHAPTER TWO

HISTORY OF THE FAMILY COURT

THE FAMILY COURT under study did not arise fully grown to be the kind of legal entity it is today. It was shaped by forces on both a local and national level. In this chapter I discuss the genesis of the family court in American society, paying particular attention to the development of the court being studied.

The Court as a Response to Social Change

The United States during the later part of the nineteenth and early twentieth centuries underwent rapid social change. The forces of urbanization and industrialization transformed the landscape of America, and by 1920 the federal census revealed that a majority of the nation's people (51.4%) lived in cities (Chudacoff: 199). Demographically, if not normatively, the city had become the center of American life. While the country continued in its course of urbanization old value structures died hard. Social fundamentalism with its emphasis on a rural, slower way of life, moral sobriety, and the self-help ethic tried to assert itself, but the industrial base of the nation continued to expand and along with it the values of consumerism and materialism.

The American family was not unaffected by these changes—increasing numbers of women entered the labor force, subtly changing the structure of the family and affecting children's socialization experiences. Technology also played a role as the automobile gave many youths hitherto undreamed of freedoms and weakened parental control.

As early as the nineteenth century, child welfare advocates were concerned about providing an environment in which children could thrive. In most instances the family provided this kind of setting, but particularly among the poor and foreign born, additional services were necessary to provide socialization and social control. A unique response to the problems which children who were labeled as deviant presented was the creation in 1899 of the first juvenile court in Cook County (Chicago). This can be viewed as a socio-legal "experiment," a unique blend of the legal and therapeutic to respond to this pressing social problem of delinquent youth. The juvenile court movement grew, and by 1925 all but two states had juvenile courts (Zukerman, 1969).

Similarly there was also concern about the impact of the changes previously mentioned upon the family. Some saw the "breakdown" of the American family as reflected in higher divorce rate, support issues, and inadequate care of children. The first family court (then called the domestic relations court) was established in New York City in 1910; this court provided for the hearing of support cases separate and apart from criminal cases.

In 1914 the first integrated family court was established in Cincinnati, Ohio. Both divorce, post-divorce matters, and juvenile cases were processed by this court. Similar courts were established in St. Louis, Missouri, in 1921; in Omaha, Nebraska, in the same year, and in Des Moines, Iowa, in 1924. In 1933 a family court which handled uncontested or default divorces was established in Milwaukee, Wisconsin.

The founding of these and similar family courts indicated the growing national concern that socio-legal matters which affected the family be responded to. However, each jurisdiction decided how domestic relations matters such as separation, divorce, custody, visitation, and paternity were to be handled. Foster (1966) indicated that the ideal family court would have comprehensive and integrated jurisdiction over all or most family problems including such matters as divorce and delinquency. The court would also employ a professional staff of psychologists, social workers, and probation officers. In the most recent article reviewing the status of family courts in the United States, Dyson and Dyson (1969) indicate that only Rhode Island and Hawaii have integrated family courts which handle the full range of socio-legal matters affecting the family. Dyson and Dyson (1969: 97) conclude that a major problem facing family courts in the nation is their generally low prestige and poor public image. Although this may still be the case, family courts and the professionals within them make far-reaching daily decisions in such matters as child custody, visitation, and support which significantly affect the course of persons involved for years to come.

The Family Court of Milwaukee County

In presenting a history of the Family Court of Milwaukee County, it is impossible for us to get an accurate picture of how services were delivered in the court, say, ten or twenty years ago. However, paying particular attention to those issues which appeared to be most important, we can see how historical factors are instrumental in shaping current practice. As Scott (1983: 169) has noted: ". . . When we observe a system at one point in time, we are seeing a cross section of elements that are the residues of diverse past experiences."

The Family Court of Milwaukee County was created by the Family Court Act of 1933. This law set up a Family Court Division within the Circuit Court to handle exclusively domestic relations cases. Robert Hansen, who served as a judge and senior judge of the Family Court in Milwaukee County from 1960-1967, authored an article on the dimensions of divorce in which he indicated that Milwaukee County was the only community in the United States which has had experience with the three major systems being used or proposed for handling divorce—"the legal-only system, the conciliation court, and the socio-legal court." (Hansen: 1966)

Prior to 1933, the founding date of the Family Court of Milwaukee County, the first of the three major systems was in place. This can be termed the "legal-only system" meaning that the courts saw their duty to grant divorces in those cases where the party "proved" that a divorce should be granted. In this system the court did little or nothing to affect reconciliation.

In 1935, the Wisconsin legislature authorized the establishment of a Family Conciliation Department (now known as Family Court Counseling Services) within the family court (Laws of Wisconsin, 1935, ch. 213. *Wis. Stat. Ann.* 252.016 Supp. 1966). Hansen (1966) dubbs this type of court "the conciliation court"; in contrast to the legal-only system, discussed earlier, the conciliation court concept tried to affect reconciliations in those cases in which reconciliation seemed likely.

Other than what has just been mentioned in terms of the court's functioning until 1960, little is known. However, in 1960, as Hanson (1966) indicates, we enter the third phase: the socio-legal family court.

The Socio-Legal Court

With the enactment of the statewide Wisconsin Family Code in the 1959 session of the Wisconsin Legislature, Wisconsin became the first state to challenge, on a statewide basis, the traditional concept that a divorce action involved no more than the spouses. Under the Wisconsin Family Code, the state and the minor children became concerned and affected parties in the divorce action, although not specifically named in the action. With the Wisconsin Family Code as the legal basis, leaders of the Family Court of Milwaukee County in the 1960's proceeded to attempt to blend the legal and therapeutic viewpoints in dealing not only with divorce but also with the welfare of children affected by divorce.

However, while not formally organized as such, the goal of blending the legal and the therapeutic within the framework of the family court was not unique to the Milwaukee court. In interviews with Judge Robert Hansen (November 27, 1984) and Judge Leander J. Foley, Jr. (September 21, 1984), two prominent leaders in the Milwaukee Family Court in the 1960's, they indicated that legal professionals in various parts of the country were concerned about the role of the courts in dealing with family disorganization. Judge Louis Burke in Denver, Judge Ben Schwartz in Cincinnati, and Judge Paul Alexander in Toledo were strong advocates of the socio-legal concept of the family court in the 1960's.

Hansen saw these influential family court judges in the 1960's as being spokesmen for what they perceived as the majority point of view in this country, that reconciliation should be attempted, that family disorganization was an adverse social factor, and that the impact of divorce upon children had to be dealt with. As Hansen stated,

> So I would say that the overwhelming majority of people in this country, every race or creed or occupation, particularly, maybe, blue collar worker types are committed for themselves and hopefully for their kids and maybe for the country to the concept of wanting marriage as a lifelong deal. (Personal Interview with Judge Robert Hansen, November 27, 1984.)

In contrast to this viewpoint, Hansen saw those in policy-influencing positions seeing "serial monogamy—the one after another, let's try again idea—as the preferable lifestyle." (Personal Interview with Judge Robert Hansen, November 27, 1984.) It was this view which family court judges opposed. Although it can be surmised that an overall goal of the family court in most communities was to endorse traditional American values regarding the family, how this goal was achieved varied from one community to another.

The Milwaukee Court and Its Leaders

Judges Hansen and Foley were the key leaders in the formation of the Family Court of Milwaukee County during the 1960's. Hansen indicated that some attorneys in Milwaukee during that time remarked that the court was a partnership between an Irish priest and a Norwegian policeman. Foley was a staunch Irish Catholic who was influenced in his work by a strong religious commitment; Hansen, on the other hand, saw himself as a pragmatist. Others may have seen him as a pragmatist also, but in addition some saw him as an individual who "ruled the family court with an iron hand," as one current family court commissioner remarked.

Through their writing in professional journals, their attendance at meetings with other family court judges, and by trying to acquaint the public with what the goals of the court were, Foley and Hansen enunciated their ideas about what the ideal family court should be and what the Milwaukee concept was. For example, Hansen authored an article on children of divorce for popular consumption in the *Reader's Digest* (March, 1967: 181-86). In that article entitled, "Children of Divorce—What Rights Have They?" he discussed the socio-legal measures which the Milwaukee Family Court took to guarantee children's rights in divorce actions. Hansen put forward a "Bill of Rights for Children in Divorce Actions" in which he indicated that children have the right to grow up in economic security, have contact with both custodial and non-custodial parents, and are entitled to periodic review of custodial arrangements and child support orders if circumstances change. Finally, Hansen stated that children involved in divorce are disadvantaged parties and that the law must take affirmative steps to protect their welfare including a social investigation, where needed, to ascertain their interests and the appointment of a lawyer-guardian (guardian ad litem) to protect their interests.

For a number of years in the 1960's the family court attempted to acquaint the local community with its work by publishing brief annual reports. The reports presented general goals of the court stressing two dominant themes of the court at the time: reconciliation and safeguarding the rights of children (see Appendix A). Statistics on cases were also presented. For example, the annual report for 1962 indicated that in that year 1,758 actions for divorce or legal separation were dismissed before trial by agreement of the parties because of lack of prosecution.

The report stated that according to the Lucas County Family Court Services of Toledo, Ohio, the national average for divorce actions initiated and subsequently dropped was 30 percent. In Milwaukee County, however, for 1962, the rate was 60 percent, meaning that for every ten actions filed, six were dropped. (From the Family Court of Milwaukee County, 1962 "Annual Report," pp. 5-6.)

The annual reports also highlighted the role of the family court commissioners, custody evaluation procedures, and the court's efforts to enforce support orders, particularly in those cases where mother and children were receiving public welfare. Finally, the annual reports stressed the idea that the family court was pervaded by a spirit of teamwork. Calling attention to this "teamwork" may simply have been an effort to advance a positive image of the court. However, it seems that the Family Court of Milwaukee in the 1960's saw itself as having a mission to help families and, to do this, enlisting support from a variety of community groups (see Appendix B).

Accomplishments of the Court in the 1960's

While the Milwaukee Family Court sought to project a positive image in terms of its work with various community segments in dealing with families, internal changes in the court to facilitate work with families also took place. Four areas of change stand out.

First, beginning in 1960, on the basis of the Wisconsin Family Code which stressed that the rights of children need to be considered in any contested custody action, the court routinely began to appoint a guardian ad litem (Latin for "guardian for the litigation"). The guardian ad litem is an attorney, appointed by the court, who acts in the best interest of the child or children in cases involving children's welfare. The attorney makes recommendations to the court in such matters as disputed custody. The practice of appointing a guardian ad litem became a well-established procedure in the court.

Second, beginning with the socio-legal court of 1960, the office of family court commissioner took on increased importance. The office of family court commissioner itself was created as part of the Family Court Act of 1933. However, prior to the appointment of Joseph Syman as the first family court commissioner in 1962 the work of the commissioner, such as pre-trial hearings and proceedings to enforce child support payments, was handled by the district attorney's office. Jeremiah Kelly was the county's divorce counsel. By 1963, the family court commissioner's office had grown to the point where there were a chief family court commissioner and three assistant commissioners.

Third, particularly in the 1960's and until no-fault divorce became a reality in Wisconsin in 1978, reconciliation was a major goal of the court. In fact, a provision of the Wisconsin Family Code required that a formal effort be made to effect reconciliation between the parties in every action of divorce or legal separation. At least one mandatory session of counseling could be obtained either privately or through the Family Conciliation Department. As a 1963 report indicated,

> A check of the cases dropped by litigants before trial discloses that 66 percent of such cases had been given personal counseling by the department. Many factors are involved in the harmonizing of domestic difficulties, but certainly the work of the department was a meaningful, helpful factor in effecting these reconciliations. (From "The Family Court of Milwaukee County 1963 Annual Report," p. 4.)

Fourth, the Milwaukee Family Court, particularly in the 1960's, saw itself as working closely with the county welfare department and private family and child welfare agencies in marriage conciliation and child custody matters. In 1963, a community resources committee consisting of education, social welfare, and religious leaders was created to form cooperative links between the court and community agencies in terms of referral and responding to unmet community needs in family matters.

The Court Under Hansen: Critics from Within

Supporters of Hansen pointed out that under his leadership the Milwaukee Family Court gained a national reputation for excellence; Hansen, however, also had his critics. Circuit Judge Robert W. Landry stated that family law in Milwaukee had become "Judge Hansen's Law." Landry was critical of the Milwaukee judicial system for allowing judges such as Hansen and Foley to dominate the work of the court (*Milwaukee Sentinel,* October 10, 1967).

Hansen had been in the family court for seven years after which time he decided to run for a justice on the Wisconsin Supreme Court. He was elected and became a justice in 1968. Foley, who had shown an interest in continuing to serve on the court after having been there for three and a half years, was assigned to another court. The Board of Circuit Court Judges voted to appoint two new judges, Marvin Holz and William Moser, to the family court for one year terms. The length of appointment of a judge to a specific court was an administrative decision. However, the decision seems to have been influenced by the view that Hansen had dominated the court for too long.

The Board of Circuit Court Judges' decision to transfer Foley to another court was met by strong objections from various persons in the community. Rabbi Louis J. Swichkow, vice-chairman of the Family Court Advisory Committee said, "I think the judges made a serious blunder in replacing Judge Foley. This is a serious mistake. This is a highly specialized field, and it isn't something one can come in on and take over for a year" (*Milwaukee Sentinel,* October 6, 1967).

In an editorial, the *Milwaukee Sentinel* (September 18, 1967) indicated,

> The transfer of Circuit Judge Leander J. Foley from the family court bench was a mistake . . . While we agree that each judge in a general court system should be able to preside over all types of cases, we also see great merit in certain judges having a specialty, especially in matters so basic and vital to our society as the family unit.

After three months as a family court judge, William Moser stated that the family court had become a legalistic jungle; he was critical of certain administrative practices of the court under Hansen. Moser stated (*Milwaukee Sentinel,* March 21, 1968), "Apparently there was an unwritten rule that attorneys could ignore the dates set for default divorces, ignore the dates at least twice without anything being said." Moser (*Milwaukee Sentinel,* March 21, 1968) also indicated that in the past the court "apparently proceeded without any formal requirements of the statutes." Moser said, "that the statutes regarding family law should be followed—as all statutes should be followed—or we should climb back in the trees." Hansen didn't comment on Moser's views. But in response to Moser's comments, Foley (*Milwaukee Sentinel,* March 21, 1968) indicated that Hansen and he made strong efforts to keep the family together when they were judges in the family court,

> If the court is oriented to the preservation of the family, you look at things one way; if you look at it strictly as a legal proceeding, I suppose you look at it another way. If we saved one marriage in 100 I think we did a service to the community.

Finally, the family court under Hansen was criticized for what was seen as a lack of productivity. On August 22, 1968, the *Milwaukee Sentinel* indicated that from January 1, 1968 to August 20, 1968, Judges Moser and Holz had disposed of 1,300 more cases than Judges Hansen and Foley had handled during the same time the previous year. There was a wide range of explanations for this phenomenon. One judge indicated that this showed that Milwaukee was on the verge of becoming a "divorce mill." When asked how he explained the great increase in the numbers of cases disposed of, Moser (*Milwaukee Sentinel,* August 22, 1968) said, "All I can say is that I come to work in the morning and I leave at the normal time at night. I don't hustle anyone in here to be divorced and no one is kicking and screaming." When hearing the statistics, Judge Foley (*Milwaukee Sentinel,* August 22, 1968) simply said, "That's unbelievable." The *Milwaukee Sentinel* (August 22, 1968) explained the differences in numbers of cases handled by indicating that Foley and Hansen did not spend as much time in the courtroom as did Moser and Holz. "Both Hansen and Foley spent considerable time on family court activities outside the courtroom, such as meetings and conferences."

Hansen had been elected to the State Supreme Court and was thus out of touch with the Milwaukee Family Court, but Judge Foley continued to be a circuit judge in Milwaukee County. Although not a family court judge, he continued to be a spokesman for the role of the court as a socio-legal entity. In a letter to his colleagues on the bench in October, 1969, he indicated that the quality of work in the court was more important than the quantity. He said that he simply could not handle family court work in the way it had been handled by Moser and Holz. Foley was also critical of the disbanding of the community resources committee that had been formed by Hansen. Foley indicated (*Milwaukee Sentinel,* September 30, 1969) that if he were able to return to the family court, the committee would be reestablished.

External Influences on the Court

Debates centering on personal conflicts, ideological differences, and organizational variations continued over the years at the family court, although the debates between Hansen and Foley and their opponents were no doubt the most lively. However, the family court was also influenced by its external environment such as legislative changes and changing family structures which called for new responses from the court.

Case decisions and legislation profoundly affected the work of the Court. For example, in April, 1972, Governor Patrick Lucey of Wisconsin signed into law a bill which substantially revised the divorce statutes. It reduced from one year to six months the waiting period for remarriage after divorce; the residency requirements for commencement of divorce actions were changed from two years to six months. The period of separation as a ground for divorce was reduced from five years to one year. Finally, the bill reduced from one year to six months the period before which the divorce became final (*Milwaukee Sentinel,* April 6, 1972).

While this bill liberalized Wisconsin's divorce laws, some attorneys felt that until Wisconsin adopted a "no fault" divorce law, its statutes would continue to be outmoded. In "no fault" divorce, the only ground necessary for divorce is that the marriage is irretrievably broken. The liberalization of divorce laws was part of a national trend. In 1973, when Hansen was State Supreme Court Justice and Foley was Chief Judge of Milwaukee County, both appeared at a forum held at a Milwaukee church. Both Foley and Hansen were dismayed with the liberalization of parts of the divorce law. Hansen (*Milwaukee Sentinel,* October 8, 1973) reiterated his belief that the courts should stress reconciliation.

However, Wisconsin became part of the national trend toward no-fault divorce when the legislature passed a no-fault divorce bill in 1977. Under the new law the single ground for divorce was a finding by the court that a marriage was irretrievably broken. According to the law, a judge could make the finding at the request of both parties, one of the parties, or if the husband and wife had voluntarily lived apart for twelve months. A major goal of no-fault divorce was to remove the need to prove one party at fault thus removing the rancor and bitterness from the proceedings. As a result of this calmer atmosphere, it was hoped that economic and custody matters would be more easily handled. With the coming of no-fault, there was an initial, dramatic increase in petitions filed for divorce and divorces granted. For example, in Milwaukee County, in 1977, the year in which no-fault legislation was passed, 4,939 petitions for divorce were filed and 4,644 divorces granted. In 1978, the first year of no-fault, 5,973 petitions for divorce were filed, and 5,114 divorces were granted. In more recent years, increases and/or decreases have been less dramatic. (See Appendix C—"Family Court Commissioner's Office, Statistics," 1978-83.)

While the public may have believed that with no-fault divorce the entire divorce process would be speeded, this was the instance in some divorce proceedings but certainly not in all. In 1978 after no-fault had been a reality for about six months, an article appeared in *The Milwaukee Journal* with the title, "Tieups Slowing Divorces in State." Although no statistics were reported, the article indicated that among the provisions of no-fault in Wisconsin which slowed the process was the fact that a court could deny a divorce or order a ninety day trial reconciliation if one of the partners successfully claimed that there was still a chance of saving the marriage. The article also pointed out that another delay built into the no-fault law was a mandatory four month wait between filing the initial petition and the final hearing to grant a divorce (*The Milwaukee Journal,* July 3, 1978).

If a major goal of the family court prior to 1978 was reconciliation, that certainly was no longer the case after 1978. After 1978, however, the court continued to reaffirm its interest and concern in matters of child custody and also child support. As part of the feminist movement, matters of child support came to the fore. In addition, public concern about rising welfare costs pressured public officials to initiate firm actions to deal with fathers who were not paying or were substantially behind on support payments. In recent years the family court has developed a complex legal-administrative framework for enforcing support payments. At times this is initiated at the county level; however, the state of Wisconsin has also become involved. In 1983, the state legislature adopted a Child Support Reform Initiative which authorized the Department of Health and Social Services to set a standard for determining child support obligations based upon a percentage of gross income and assets and will eventually have a mandatory payroll deduction plan for payment of support.

The matter of child custody remains a thorny socio-legal issue. The guideline, "What is in the best interest of the child?" is difficult to decide. New forms of custody as in joint custody, preclude either parent from automatically gaining custody. The case of *Milliken vs. Milliken* (Wisconsin Statutes, 1982) pointed out that custody cannot be readily changed, in fact, it can be changed only if it is in the best interest of the child. Thus, the court probably is spending extra time in making these often difficult decisions.

The Work Environment of the Contemporary Court

If the major tasks facing the court have changed somewhat over the years, it appears that its organizational structure has also changed. In an interview (May 15, 1984), Judge Robert Curley who was a family court judge for several years in the 1960's, chief judge in Milwaukee County for four years, and presiding judge in the family court for three years from 1980-83 before his retirement, discussed his view of bureaucracy in the courts.

> When I first became a judge in 1960 I was responsible to the Wisconsin State Supreme Court. When I left 23 years later, I was responsible to the Wisconsin State Supreme Court, the State Court Administrator, the Deputy State Court Administrator, the head of the Judicial Ethics Committee, the head of the Judicial Education Committee, the Chief Judge in my own jurisdiction, the Deputy Chief Judge, the Deputy State Court Administrator in my own jurisdiction, and the Presiding Judge of my division. This bureaucracy didn't exist when I became a judge in 1960. I think a lot of the bureaucracy is make-work for people . . . it's created jobs. (Personal Interview with Judge Robert Curley, May 15, 1984.)

In viewing his twenty-three years on the bench, Curley felt that the court system had become overburdened, and that as a result people were not given quality decisions. Further, he stated (Personal Interview with Judge Robert Curley, May 5, 1984), "If you [the court] didn't have commissioners and social workers, the whole system would break down."

A case can be made for the view that the family court as an organization has become amorphous. A listing of the goals of the court, as formulated in the Hansen years could not be found in the current court. A statement made in an interview with Bob Frances (Personal Interview with Bob Frances, November 28, 1984), a senior social worker at the court, however, is noteworthy: "It's [the family court] not an organization, it's four judges, eight commissioners, and seven social workers doing their own thing."

Susan Samson, the current Chief Family Court Judge, sees a major role of the court as educating the persons who appear before it as to what the law means. "I have to do a lot of explaining to people. This is a high volume court. It's set up to deal with people with brevity. I feel I have a duty to explain things. This slows me down." (Personal Interview with Judge Susan Samson, September 21, 1984.)

Newspaper reports of activities of the court in the 1960's and 1970's highlighted individual personalities and conflicts among judges and legal changes and their impact on the court. In more recent years, since 1980, not much attention has been paid to the judges. An exception to this is the case of Judge George Alexander who was the subject of the Wisconsin Judicial Commission's investigation for unethical conduct (*The Milwaukee Journal,* November 22, 1984).

However, Milwaukee's major newspapers continued to report legal changes and their impact on the operation of the court. For example, on July 4, 1981, the *Milwaukee Sentinel* reported that a new state law required closed hearings in paternity cases; under the new law paternity cases are purely civil rather than quasi-criminal in nature. In addition, the new law provided that custody and visitation terms be set at the time support payments are determined, thus extending more rights to the father.

While the family court of Milwaukee County no longer seems to be a major news item, in 1982, from August 15-19, a *Milwaukee Journal* reporter wrote a series on the work of the court, focusing in particular on the work of the judges and commissioners (he did not look at what social workers do). Although this series by Gary Rummler is not an investigation by a social scientist, but rather by a journalist, the series is worth mentioning.

Rummler presented a series of case vignettes—description of cases usually involving divorce, custody, and support—which he observed being presented to judges and commissioners. Woven throughout were biographical descriptions of judges and commissioners and some details of administrative matters as salaries, years of service, and case appeals. Rummler (1982) described one assistant court commissioner as being "all business":

> She is a no-nonsense commissioner when it comes to getting money from fathers for their children. She told one father, who was angry over the support payments that he had been ordered to pay, that his child should be more important than the 1980 car he was making payments on. And in another case, in which she advised the wife not to let her husband fail to meet his obligations, she said: "You should remember he is divorcing you, not the children." (*The Milwaukee Journal,* August 17, 1982.)

Rummler also sketched out some details of the physical environment, somewhat facetiously:

> The first thing you notice in the family court commissioner's waiting room is that this is not a place where males and females sit together. Unless one happens to be a lawyer . . . You can tell which ones are the lawyers. They are the happy ones. After all, nearly everyone else is losing wages by being here. (*The Milwaukee Journal,* August 15, 1982.)

Granted, this is not social science analysis, but it is a journalistic attempt to make some sense out of an organization and what it is all about. Professionals, their cases, routines, the environment predominate; the primary work is to process people. Formal, rational organization as it impacts on professional decision making is not in evidence, but professional discretion in the interpretation of law is clearly present.

The view which emerges of the current family court is that of a highly complex, though amorphous organizational structure in which professionals operate with autonomy and substantial discretion within an atmosphere of time constraints and somewhat limited manpower. Essentially this is Lipsky's (1980) view of a street-level bureaucracy.

The Approach

A brief historical overview of the Family Court in Milwaukee County has just been presented. The court is a complex legal organization which over the years has been influenced by both historical and institutional factors. Internally the court's purpose and structure have been shaped by its leaders, the judges, whose ideological viewpoints and at times personal conflicts with peers have shaped what the court has done. Historical and institutional forces have had a great impact upon the court; in family law as seen in new laws enacted by the legislature and case decisions. In addition, county government and its concern that the court be fiscally responsible especially in enforcing support also has made its presence felt. Local newspapers which often see themselves as "watchdogs" of the court are also there. Finally, social and cultural forces as seen in the changing American family and changing gender roles, have also been influential in terms of custody and support issues.

Apparent in the history of the Family Court of Milwaukee County is an emerging desire for organizational wholeness or rationality as is seen in the controversies described in this chapter. The court under the "Irish priest and Norwegian policeman" believed that a good disposition was reconciliation, that the child was best served through an intact marriage, and that the law itself was best served when these results were achieved. However, this description or account of the court was based on the premise that reconciliation in many cases was possible and that the court should direct its resources toward that goal. Widespread social changes as reflected in no-fault divorce made it easier for persons to put an end to a marriage rather than to try to patch it up. Interest in the welfare of children affected by divorce continued, however, in spite of the fact that the court was no longer primarily one of reconciliation.

There is ample evidence to indicate that once the court was no longer one of reconciliation, it did not regain any sense of overall organizational rationality. Yet its work continued and it processed large numbers of persons as it attempted to deal with a complexity of issues while lacking any sense of moral order. Professionals were responsible for making decisions, but they went about doing their work in an organization which seemed to lack any overall purpose. But exactly how do professionals go about doing their work in a complex yet seemingly amorphous organization? How can they make sense out of their work lives in light of these organizational gaps between what is and what is supposed to be, between the ideal and the real? It is primarily these questions which this study seeks to answer. However, before these questions can be addressed, the theoretical framework which guides this study needs to be examined. This is the focus of the next chapter.

CHAPTER THREE

THE PROBLEM: ACCOUNTING FOR ORGANIZATIONAL DISCREPANCIES

AS HAS JUST been discussed, there have been efforts throughout the history of the court to achieve organizational wholeness or rationality, an overall organizational design and mission. This is evident, for example, in the efforts of Judge Hansen in the 1960's to achieve a blend of the legal and therapeutic ideologies and integrate them into the operation of the court. However, while this was being attempted, both the legal and social work professions were developing what can be termed rational accounting practices, procedures that helped each member make his/her work in the court manageable. Sometimes this merged with broad organizational goals, at other times not.

In this chapter the basic problem of the study is presented—accounting for organizational discrepancies, the effort to resolve the continual tension between the historical aim for overall design, on the one hand, and particular, ("street-level") organizational articulations, on the other. The problem is not a new one. Three frameworks that address it are presented: the formal/rational model, the social construction approach, and the institutional approach. By means of data from the family court, in subsequent chapters it is shown how elements from all three approaches need to be used for understanding the dynamics of organizational discrepancies. A key concept of the social construction view centers on the discussion of accounts. It is suggested that different street-level bureaucrats or professionals within the court, depending on their particular work role and function, will present differing accounts and resolve the problem of organizational discrepancies in particular and practical ways, not in some overall formal/rational mode.

The Formal/Rational Model

In 1922 Max Weber formulated what is still the most influential statement and the point of departure for the analysis of formal organizations. The terms "formal organization" and "bureaucracy" are closely related; in fact, Merton (1968) refers to the ideal type of formal organization as bureaucracy. Shafritz and Whitbeck (1978: 1) indicate that the hallmark of classical organization theory is "a concern for organizational structure that is premised upon the assumed rational behavior of its human parts."

Another aspect of the formal/rational model is the strong emphasis placed on organizational goals. Specific goals are formulated, and organizational participants are expected to achieve them; discrepancies occur when the goals are not achieved, as the result of inter-goal competition or compromise. Using these principles of goal direction, rational behavior within a monolithic organization, theorists working within the formal/rational framework have produced numerous organizational studies. For example, Barnard's (1938) interest in conscious coordination of activities parallels Weber's interest in the systematic division of tasks and authority in the rational control of performance. As Barnard (1938: 4) states, "Formal organization is that kind of cooperation that is conscious, deliberate, purposeful."

Later, Parsons (1960) defined an organization as a social system that focuses on the attainment of a specific goal and contributes, in turn, to the goals of a more comprehensive system, such as society itself. March and Simon (1958) viewed organizations as rationally arranged situations designed for specific purposes. Etzioni (1969) in his analysis of complex organizations, saw the central variable for characterizing differences among them as the relationship between those in charge and those under control. Etzioni claimed that the means of control is so essential in organizations that organizations which differ on the control dimension differ on most others.

Numerous empirical studies have been done using the formal organization framework; several have focused primarily on goals and their impact on organizational functioning. A classical study in this genre is Michel's (1969) work on political parties. In addition, Seeley (1957) studied voluntary associations (the Community Chest), and Belkamp (1956) described the working of mental hospitals. These studies show that organizations do not consistently realize their goals in an efficient manner and also that the organization frequently has different goals than those which it states.

Legal organizations, in particular those dealing with criminal justice, have been studied using the formal/rational framework. Much research has centered on the formal rules of the organization and how rationality can be increased by minimizing discretion, for example, by precisely specifying the roles of members (Goldstein, 1960).

Another major object of empirical studies using the formal/rational model as a framework has been to measure organizational effectiveness by contrasting observed, actual behavior with the stated, formal goals of the organization. An example of this type of research is Lefstein, Stapleton, and Teitelbaum's (1969) study of judges' compliance to the *Gault* decision. The *Gault* decision, rendered in 1967, involved a case in which a boy had been sentenced to a long term in a correctional institution without proper provision of due process. The United States Supreme Court heard the case and affirmed the need to apply the provisions of the Bill of Rights to cases involving juvenile delinquents (Cavan, 1969: 414-415). Lefstein, Stapleton, and Teitelbaum's (1969) study demonstrated that in various jurisdictions and types of cases, judges' conformity to the *Gault* decision varied. Feeley (1973) indicates that this study did not examine the wide variety of factors, goals, and incentives which affect individual judges and their differential interpretation of the *Gault* decision.

> A skeptical social scientist might well ask of a lower court judge, "So the Supreme Court handed down a decision, why should it affect you?" A full analysis of the dynamics of compliance and a theory of organization effectiveness would have to address itself to this question which assumes that the Supreme Court decision is just one of a number of factors affecting the system (Feeley, 1973).

As Feeley implies, individual justices were judged in terms of their success in applying the general ruling, not in terms of their "street-level" rationality.

Two other, similar studies examined the impact of the *Miranda* decision on police behavior (Wald, 1966: Medalie, R. J., 1968). In the *Miranda* decision, the Supreme Court held that the police must give a suspect certain warnings before subjecting him or her to custodial questioning. In studies of the decision, the requirements specified in the decision are regarded as the formal goals. The actual behavior of the police is studied and contrasted with the formal goals specified in the decision. The studies report a generally low compliance level to the decision on the part of the police and speculate that this might be due to the newness of the decision or hostility on the part of the police to the requirements of the *Miranda* decision. However, as in the study on *Gault* mentioned earlier, no effort was made to systematically examine the wide range of factors (alternate, reasonable goals) that might explain the low level of compliance on the part of the police. To do this, what is necessary is a research perspective which espouses a dynamic model of organizational life—one which is constantly influenced by both internal and external factors.

In summary, the formal/rational model views organizations as rationally contrived units of human association. The organization is seen as a monolithic, unitary entity the goals of which are clear; organizational discrepancies become apparent when the organization does not achieve its goals. To deal with organizational discrepancies, limits are set on individual actions and actors by a controlling group. This unidimensional view of the organization appears to place an undue emphasis on formal goals and means without sufficiently considering other factors which are perhaps equally as important in shaping the behavior and effectiveness of actors within the organization.

The Social Construction Framework

If Weber is the pioneer spokesman for the formal/rational model, Peter Berger and Thomas Luckmann (1966) in *The Social Construction of Reality* set forth a key statement of what will be referred to as the social construction framework. While Berger and Luckmann were concerned primarily with the role of knowledge in society, their investigation of the social processes whereby knowledge is created has relevance for understanding the behavior of organizational members. In this framework organizations are seen as complexes of social interactions in the process of creation; in essence, organizations are "ongoing concerns" (Hughes, 1971). Instead of unidimensional rationality, as in the Weberian approach, the social construction framework sees the organization as composed of "rationalizing" processes-activities that give meaning to or make reasonable the objects and events of a particular domain of everyday life. As will be discussed later in detail, this study is particularly concerned with the differing forms of rationality that suit particular work roles and functions within the organization.

Appearing a year later than Berger and Luckmann's work was Garfinkel's *Studies in Ethnomethodology* (1967). Berger and Luckmann (1966) stressed that man externalizes his existence in objectifications (society), while simultaneously being subjectively emergent from the boundaries of these objectifications. Garfinkel (1967) went on to demonstrate through a number of ethnomethodological "experiments" that the social order itself is tenuous, continually emergent and at the same time "reasoned out." This approach focuses on the ongoing process of reality construction that comes about from the activity of actors in carrying on their everyday life. The interactional processes by which social worlds are maintained have also been thoroughly described by Goffman (1967).

The literature which examines how professionals in organizations go about doing their work, and in the process construct rationality, is still somewhat sparse. Cicourel et al., (1974) described the work of teachers in an elementary school, Garfinkel (1967) studied the process whereby records are constructed in psychiatric clinics, and Buckholdt and Gubrium (1979) studied the social organization of the treatment of emotionally disturbed children in a residential treatment center.

One of the most widely read works on legal organizations using this framework is Jerome Skolnick's (1966). His book, *Justice Without Trial,* could also be called "doing justice"; it is an analysis of the functioning of the police in law enforcement. However, it also deals with police-prosecutor-court relationships and indicates that these relationships are part of a complex bargaining and exchange system involving competing senses of the overall organization of judicial affairs of which they are a part—hardly a unitary vision of things.

In another well-known study, Sudnow (1965) discusses the interrelationships between public prosecutor, public defender, and defendant in the matter of plea bargaining. By studying transcripts of the actual interchanges among participants in the system, Sudnow indicates that the achievement of multiple oganizational goals as avoidance of trial, on the one hand, and "justice" (or retribution), on the other, is a delicate balancing act.

> Both P.D. [Public Defender] and D.A. [District Attorney] are concerned to obtain a guilty plea wherever possible and thereby avoid a trial. At the same time, each party is concerned that the defendant "receive his due." The reduction of offense X to Y must be of such a character that the new sentence will depart from the anticipated sentence for the original charge to such a degree that the defendant is likely to plead guilty to the new charge and, at the same time, not so great that the defendant does not "get his due." (Sudnow, 1965: 262)

Cicourel (1976) studied how juvenile delinquents were processed by the juvenile justice system. In field studies of two police and probation departments and juvenile court operations, Cicourel documented, by using verbatim conversations or reports whenever possible, the social processes whereby delinquency is constructed.

Street-Level Bureaucracy as a Social Construction

One of the hallmarks of modern Western society has been the proliferation of formal organizations specifically designed to provide human services to cope with problems of daily living. In *Asylums: Essays on the Social Situation of Mental Patients and Other Inmates,* Goffman (1961) concentrated on conceptualizing an extreme form of such organizations. Since that time numerous studies have been done that examine how organizational structures affect the fate of the people they serve. Recent works, particularly in medical sociology, which deal with this theme are Levine's (1980) *From State Hospital to Psychiatric Center,* Morrissey, Goldman, and Klerman's (1980) *The Enduring Asylum: Cycles of Institutional Reform at Worcester State Hospital,* Gubrium and Buckholdt's (1982) *Describing Care* and Gubrium's (1975) *Living and Dying at Murray Manor.*

Increasing attention, however, is being paid to those organizations whose explicit function is not to directly change the behavior of people but rather to process and confer public statuses on them. Examples are a diagnostic clinic, a university admissions office, a juvenile court, a credit bureau, and a welfare office. Hasenfeld (1972) developed a theoretical framework for analyzing people-processing organizations. Using a social exchange frame of reference, Hasenfeld contended that the core technology of people-processing organizations is the classification and disposition of clients. Initially clients are placed somewhere in the organizational network, given services, and then discharged with a different status (in the case of the family court, for example, the status of "divorced"). In order to accomplish its tasks, these organizations employ persons who are what Hasenfeld refers to as "boundary actors." In this position, the service provider has control over the exigencies of the organization in terms of service provision but also has monopolistic control of knowledge regarding the client's condition. The autonomy of the bureaucrat is evident since he alone in the organization has knowledge of both client and organizational requirements.

Hasenfeld (1972: 262) indicates that he did not examine in depth the role of the service provider in these organizations but that this needs to be done. This is certainly the case when the basic concepts of people-processing organizations are used to analyze the role of the bureaucrat in public service bureaucracies. The role of these service providers is worth examining. Prottas (1977: 1) indicated that in 1972 the federal, state, and local government of the United States employed over 9.5 million people in the five primary areas of public service: education, policing, welfare, health, and employment security. The majority of these people work in bureaucracies whose responsibility it is to distribute a public good—health care, money, or justice. Not only are a significant number of man-hours involved in public service bureaucracies, but the amount of public money involved is also substantial.

Given the scale of these public services, it is not surprising that academicians have turned their attention to the study of public service bureaucracies. As noted in the Preface, Lipsky (1973: 196) coined the term "street-level bureaucrat" to describe "public service workers who interact directly with citizens in the course of their jobs, and who have substantial discretion in the execution of their work." In addition to Lipsky's work on street-level bureaucracy, Jeffrey Prottas (1979), a political scientist, as Lipsky, authored *People Processing: The Street-Level Bureaucrat in Public Service Bureaucracies.* In this book Prottas detailed the work of bureaucrats such as an intake welfare worker, a public housing manager, a clerk at the Veterans Administration Hospitals' Out-Patient Department, and an emergency room clerk at a hospital. While these occupations are different, they encounter similar conditions of work in terms of limited resources, the need to process cases, and the task of developing coping strategies for accomplishing the tasks at hand. The role of the street-level bureaucrat has a number of characteristics. First, the street-level bureaucrat must cope with a large caseload and often impose standardized ways of dealing with the individual. At its worst, this kind of "mass processing" can lead to routinizing, favoritism, and stereotyping (Prottas, 1979). Second, the organizations for which street-level bureaucrats work have goals which are at times ambiguous and sometimes contradictory. Third, organizations provide limited resources so that frequently clients are not adequately served; the street-level bureaucrat must offer explanations for this to the client—a task which is often emotionally demanding (e.g. explaining eligibility requirements to applicants who are denied public assistance).

In formulating the concept of street-level bureaucracy, Lipsky has created an ideal type. A major problem with the conceptual work of both Lipsky and Prottas is that their concept conflates too many types of people servers who have obvious differences. To paraphrase Wilensky

(1964), it is tantamount to the street-level bureaucratization of everyone—from teachers, social workers, judges, police, to intake welfare workers, public housing managers, and emergency room clerks.

However, if carefully specified and elaborated, it is suggested that the concept of street-level bureaucracy is a most useful one to apply to the family court. One of the perennial problems of the court has been the need to process people at a relatively rapid rate due in part to limited manpower. In addition, while the goals of the court may have been somewhat clear in the 1960's they no longer seem to exist. Finally, discrepancies in the form of problems within the family court as an organization seem to abound (e.g. differing ideologies, organizational contradictions, personal views) and yet the bureaucrats must live and work in this kind of atmosphere. Obviously these are all characteristics of a street-level bureaucracy, as noted by Lipsky (1980).

While Lipsky and Prottas have described the work role of the bureaucrats they studied, they have not paid sufficient attention to differences between street-level bureaucrats of different professions within the same organization. In this investigation I will deal with this matter. Finally, I am most interested in how street-level bureaucrats/professionals go about socially constructing their work role and rationality. They have considerable autonomy by nature of their organizational position to do this—to make their work life manageable so that organizational problems can be dealt with.

The Institutional Framework

Perrow (1979: 199) calls the institutional school the most sociological of all schools of organizational theory. This school has spawned numerous organizational studies, many of which have used structural-functionalism as the major conceptual framework. In this view functions determine the structure of organizations and organizational structures in turn can be understood by analyzing their functions.

The emphasis of research of this school has been on the well-documented case study in which the organization is analyzed as a whole in order to capture its organic character. However, specific organizational processes are also analyzed in detail and once again related to the whole. The classic work using this type of approach is Selznick's (1949) case study, *TVA and the Grass Roots.* Selznick found that the Tennessee Valley Authority's rubric of grass-roots involvement and control in recreation, forestry, and farming programs led to control of the agency on the part of powerful local and national interests and the eventual subversion of agency goals by institutional processes.

As discussed earlier in this chapter (see p. 32), the formal/rational model stresses the importance of stated organizational goals. While the institutional school recognizes the importance of formal goals, it also examines in detail deviations from these goals. Dalton (1959) analyzed several commercial and industrial firms including middle-sized and large factories, a department store, and a research firm. Dalton views organizational structures as not fixed but as shifting phases of action, employed by management, to attain stated goals. Gouldner (1954) in his study of a midwestern gypsum plant analyzed how this plant became a rational-legal bureaucracy and the clash with community values which resulted.

Human service organizations have also come under analysis of the institutional school. Scott (1967) in his study of agencies which attempt to rehabilitate the blind, found that stated agency goals to help "the blind" really meant "the desirable blind," typically young people who have some employment prospects. However, there were not enough "desirable blind" to go around and so agencies had to compete with one another for clients. They then attempted to keep the young blind dependent on the agency rather than assist them to achieve self sufficiency—the agency's professed goal. Perrow (1961) showed how the stated research goals of a private hospital became subverted when donors insisted that money given be used only for elaborate electronic gadgetry. Street, Vinter, and Perrow (1966) described how treatment goals often become subordinated to the economic demands of the organization and the influence of powerful professional groups in the organization.

The institutional school also stresses the importance of understanding an organization's history in order to illuminate contemporary events. Messinger (1955) discussed the historical events which culminated in the Townsend Organization, and similarly Gusfield (1955) showed how historical events reshaped the goals of the Women's Christian Temperance Union. Zald and Denton (1963) showed how the YMCA (Young Men's Christian Association) was transformed from an organization which helped poor immigrants to one which became oriented toward providing recreational outlets for middle-class youth. Neither the formal/rational model nor social construction model considered earlier in this chapter shows the same interest in the importance of tracing the history of a specific organization in order to comprehend its current functioning.

The major contribution of the institutional school, according to Perrow (1979: 198), was the attempt to understand the organization's relationship to its environment. The formal/rational model has focused attention on the organization's internal environment. Weber specified that the work of an organization be conducted on a continuous basis, that there be a hierarchy of offices, and a division of labor specifying the amount of power or authority an individual has. The performance of duties was governed by written rules. The social construction model has also focused attention on the internal environment not so much in terms of the factors which Weber presented, but more in terms of how participants actively construct the organizational work environment to convince one another that the social world makes sense.

The institutional model takes into consideration both the internal and external environments of the organization. Human patterns of organization are seen as existing at different system levels, from micro units among individuals to macro forms of collective organization, as institutions. It is necessary to understand the historical and present relationships among these various levels of organizations.

The different organizational schools discussed in this chapter can be viewed as efforts to describe and analyze how the matter of social order is organizationally dealt with. Since the construction of social order is above all a human enterprise it is necessary to consider how human actors within an organization go about dealing with discrepancies, gaps between the real and the ideal, to achieve order. It is this matter which will now be discussed.

Accounts

Part of the genius of Weber along with other classical sociologists such as Durkheim and Marx was that each made overtures to deal with both micro and macro levels of sociological analysis. For example, Weber dealt with such macro variables as the state, capitalism, and bureaucracy; at the same time he espoused the viewpoint that it was essential, through the study of social action, to analyze the meaningful action of individuals as affected by social structures. In the case of bureaucracy, Weber's statement on the subject deals with analysis on the macro level. I am suggesting that to understand the functioning of bureaucrats, the meaning of specific types of encompassing and "lived" (Schutz, 1970) social structures also needs to be explored.

Sociologists have developed several concepts for dealing with the problem of how actors restore disrupted meaning, repair fractured social interaction, and renegotiate identity issues; how persons deal with social structure. The basis for much work in this area in sociology was C. Wright Mills' (1940) statement on "vocabularies of motive" which will be examined in detail shortly. Hall and Hewitt (1970) put forth the concept of "quasi-theories"—explanations which people construct in social interactions to account for various kinds of problematic situations. The concept of the disclaimer, an interactional tactic used by actors to neutralize an upcoming disruptive event is explored by Hewitt and Stokes (1975), and Scott and Lyman (1968) developed the concept of accounts.

All of these concepts can be viewed as "aligning actions" (Hewitt and Stokes, 1975) which social actors use to preserve situational definitions in the face of disruptive conduct. By the use of these actions, culture enters individual action, and social order and continuity is maintained. This study is most interested in one type of aligning action—that of accounts.

The term "account" has been used in several ways by sociologists. An account resembles the concept of "motive" in Weber's sense of the term. Weber defined a motive "as a complex of subjective meaning which seems to the actor himself or to the observer as adequate ground for the conduct in question." (Weber, 1947: 98-99)

Using a social action approach, Mills (1940) argued that motives are words but do not denote any element "within" individuals; rather, they stand for anticipated situational consequences of questioned conduct. Further, motives used in justifying or criticizing an act link the act to situations and integrate one individual's action with another's, aligning conduct with norms. Working vocabularies of motive, rooted in language and social action, have "careers that are woven through changing institutional fabrics." (Mills, 1940: 908)

Expanding on Mills' ideas, Scott and Lyman (1968), in an essay simply titled "Accounts" contended that the fundamental feature of human relations is talk. They dealt with one feature of talk:

> Its ability to shore up the timber of fractured sociation, its ability to throw bridges between the promised and the performed, its ability to repair the broken and restore the estranged. (Scott and Lyman, 1968: 46)

This involves the giving and receiving of accounts. According to Scott and Lyman (1968: 46), an account is "a statement made by a social actor to explain unanticipated or untoward behavior—whether the proximate cause for the statement arises from the actor himself or from someone else." Constructs such as accounts are crucial elements in maintaining social order since they prevent conflict from arising by bridging the gap between events and expectations. In other words, the use of accounts rationalizes ongoing conduct. The importance of accounts is reiterated by Ritzer (1975: 117): ". . . it is in the accounts (actors' explanations of their actions) of these actors that the experience and maintenance of social structure is revealed."

According to Scott and Lyman (1968: 47) there are basically two types of accounts: justifications and excuses. However, in a broad sense accounts can also be seen as explanations; much of what is true about accounts will also hold for explanations. Justifications are accounts in which one accepts responsibility for the stated act but denies any guilt associated with it. For example, an individual may bomb an abortion clinic, since he believes that "killing the unborn" is wrong. Excuses are accounts in which one admits that the matter in question is wrong or bad but denies full responsibility. For example, a parent who beat his infant child for screaming may admit that this is wrong but add, "After a rough day at work I just couldn't stand my child's screaming." Scott and Lyman (1948: 49) go on to discuss various types of excuses based on biological drives, accidents, and scapegoating.

Accounts may or may not be honored. A key variable governing the honoring of an account is the social group, culture, or subculture in which the account is introduced. For example, organizations routinely provide accounts for their members to use in a variety of situations. These accounts "work" because of existing tacit background acceptances of the persons involved. For example, the client accepts the decision of the bureaucrat when she is told that her income level makes her ineligible for food stamps, since "everybody knows" that people have to follow the rules and that an account such as the one offered is acceptably reasonable under the circumstances.

Accounts are also produced in a variety of linguistic styles; Scott and Lyman (1968: 55) mention five: intimate, casual, consultative, formal, and frozen styles. For instance, the casual style is used among peers, insiders, and in-group members. The formal style is used when persons are in rigidly defined statuses, as a judge and defendant in a courtroom. The frozen style is an extreme example of the formal style—e.g. interaction between a pilot and an air traffic controller.

A key element in accounts is that they always occur between persons in roles—between doctor and patient, judge and defendant, teacher and student. A normative structure governs the giving and receiving of accounts including what accounts are given, honored, or discredited. Scott and Lyman (1968: 59) indicate that "every account is a manifestation of the underlying negotiation of identities."

Accounts can be seen as the means whereby problems are dealt with—explained, justified, or excused by street-level bureaucrats or professionals. By studying accounts one learns how actors put together a world view which explains organizational difficulties or at least how these accounts help the individual live with the difficulties. In essence, accounts are the building blocks of rationality.

A Typology of Accounts

It has been shown that differing accounts are used by diverse actors in a variety of social situations. One device for organizing accounts presented by actors in an organization is by means of a typology. As Williamson, Karp, and Dolphin (1977: 47) point out, a typology is a systematic organizing device which enables the researcher to see the underlying or basic dimensions of the data. While preliminary data collection may help formulate elements of the typology, theoretical considerations also shape the form which the typology takes.

While Hasenfeld (1972), Prottas (1979), and Lipsky (1980) have discussed the theoretical rationale specifically for the street-level bureaucracy framework, elements of this framework can be applied to a wide range of human service organizations. The street-level bureaucrat in his/her work role is continually dealing with three elements of organizational work life which in turn shape the accounts which are presented. First, persons within the organization serve as a basis for accounts; references are made to people which shape the organizational role of the service provider. However, persons external to the organization who influence the street-level bureaucrat in his/her role also serve as the basis for accounts. Second, internal-organizational factors, referents to the organization *per se* also serve as the basis for accounts. There is also an external dimension to these accounts in which organizations other than the organization itself are used as a means by which the bureaucrat explains organizational work life. Third, internal-ideological factors, a world view specific to the street-level bureaucracy itself, can be called on as a basis for accounts. As with both personal and organizational accounts, ideological accounts also have an external dimension; external-ideological accounts with their basis in the broader culture, for example, can be called upon as a basis for accounts. Therefore it is suggested that one typology which has relevance for understanding service provision in human service organizations is the following:

A Typology of Accounts

	Internal	External
Personal	I	II
Organizational	III	IV
Ideological	V	VI

This typology can be used to understand the social organization of accounts in a variety of organizational settings; examples of how it can be used follow.

For five years I was on the staff of a residential treatment center for emotionally disturbed children. This center provided twenty-four hour a day, five day per week care for children between the ages of six and thirteen who were diagnosed as being emotionally disturbed. On weekends, these children were sent home to their families to maintain familial contact, since after the average eighteen-month placement the children would once again live with their families. While at the center the children attended school, received individual counseling, and lived in cottages with peers. The treatment team, as it was called, consisted of a teacher, a social worker, and a child care worker who supervised the children in their cottage. An average of sixty children were in residence at any given time; five full-time teachers, five social workers, and five child care workers in addition to part-time workers and a small administrative staff were responsible for treatment programs for the children. The major task of the professional staff was to devise and implement specific treatment programs for each child. There was considerable interaction among the staff consisting of meetings to discuss progress of the children, problem areas, and professional roles. A program requirement was that the progress of each child be reviewed every six months by the staff in consultation with a psychiatrist or psychologist. This was a standard of the funding agency, in this case, the county which paid for the cost of care for the children, and which also expected ongoing assessments of the child's progress.

In this organization, as in others, accounts are used to bridge the gap between the real and the ideal, in matters of conduct and treatment. Consider, first, the use of an internal-personal account, meaning a personal account about someone within the organization, to "explain away" deviation from organizational rules.

A speech therapist complains that a teacher does not send a certain child from her classroom to the speech therapist on time. The speech therapist's account: "I wish she would send Joel to speech therapy on time, but I guess I shouldn't get upset. With all the acting-out children in her classroom, it's easy to lose track of time and forget."

Thus, with this account the speech therapist bridges the gap between a formally functioning organization and its requirements for adherence to time limits and the demands of the individual case the deviance of which oversteps these formal time requirements.

Sometimes the funding agency, the county, was reluctant to permit children to remain in treatment because of financial considerations; however, the staff may have felt that a longer time was necessary to make the child's treatment complete. A staff member disagreed with the county's decision and expressed this at a staffing, and in doing so legitimated the ideology of altruism, as opposed to the viewpoint which sees cases primarily in terms of economics. For example,

> David (the child in treatment) has made good progress here, but he's really not quite ready to leave. I guess the county looks at dollars and cents; they really don't understand that this kid is still struggling and to send him home to a shaky family situation could cause him to regress.

Ideological differences also influenced children's treatment at the center. At a staffing, a social worker who was seeing the child in individual therapy sessions and the consulting psychiatrist discussed ways of assisting the child to handle his anger more effectively. The social worker argued that discussing with the child his anger, as expressed in recent episodes and exploring with him alternate ways of handling his feelings, were the most effective ways to deal with the problem. The psychiatrist argued differently:

> Bob has had a very traumatic early childhood—rejection by his own parents and then placement in a number of foster homes. The psychogentic roots of his anger are obviously there, and I think a major goal of therapy needs to be assisting the child to recognize his repressed anger, particularly toward authority figures and helping him to work through these feelings with his therapist.

A discussion ensued and a compromise was reached, incorporating both strategies in one approach. As argued by the psychiatrist, not only was he commenting on Bob, an emotionally disturbed boy, but he was doing organizational work at the same time, rationalizing a type of organizational discrepancy by means of an ideological account.

The foregoing are examples of accounts used by service providers in a human service organization. On the basis of repeated observations of and interviews with these persons, a picture of their work within the organization and the social structure of the organization itself emerges. One may find, for example, that some professions, as social work, may be predominantly involved in internal-ideological accounts, whereas child care workers may be more involved in internal-personal accounts.

Roles and the Articulation of Differential Types

Lipsky (1980) and Prottas (1979) in their work on street-level bureaucracy view it as a unitary phenomenon and assume that street-level bureaucrats in a variety of settings look at their work in similar ways. However, when the research on professional roles is reviewed, it is seen to be a complex phenomenon in which the organizational setting greatly influences professional role performance. Hall (1973), in a review article, "Theoretical Trends in the Sociology of Professions" indicates that professional/bureaucratic roles are heavily influenced by the organizations in which their work takes place. In view of this, ecological models have been developed to further assess professional and bureaucratic work environments (Aldrich and Pfeffer, 1976, and Hall, 1982). In spite of these research studies, Kerr and his associates (1977) point out that professional roles are still hard to define. Different professions possess and make use to varying degrees these six commonly held characteristics of "ideal" professionals: expertise, autonomy, commitment, identification with the profession and fellow professionals, ethics, and collegial standards.

Based on the above, one would expect to find judges, family court commissioners, and social workers to make use of differing types of accounts to make sense out of their organizational work. In the following three chapters the accounts of professionals in their work are discussed.

CHAPTER FOUR

JUDGES AND THEIR WORK

The Setting

THE FAMILY COURT of Milwaukee County is located in the Milwaukee County Courthouse in downtown Milwaukee. The courthouse itself is a large, imposing structure, of Grecian architecture, orginally constructed in 1926. Since that time additions, in the form of an annex which spans an abutting freeway and interior building changes have taken place. Although a variety of both internal and external physical changes have occurred over the years, what remains is the imposing character of the building. Wide marble corridors, vaulted ceilings, ornate woodwork, and the massive character of granite seem to state that there is something enduring about the law and institutions which embody it. Signs in various parts of the courthouse remind one that this is an official place. A sign near a courtroom states, "Silence, Courts in Session"; on a door near Family Court Counseling Services a sign states, "Authorized Personnel Only."

The family court complex is located on the seventh floor of the courthouse. There are the offices of the Family Court Commissioner, Deputy Court Commissioner, and assistant court commissioners along with administrative and clerical personnel. Adjoining these offices are the offices of the Family Court Counseling Services, the social workers, and clerical personnel. Across the hall, on either end of the floor are two courtrooms for family court judges; two additional family courtrooms are located on the third and fifth floors.

The judge, by virtue of the legal power ascribed to him, is the most powerful individual in the family court. While the family court commissioner is responsible for handling pre-judgment orders regarding family matters, the judge makes final judgments—in Milwaukee County, for example, he alone can grant a divorce. Judges are still held in generally high regard by the general public, but also within the court, judges are held in high esteem because of the matters with which they deal. As one assistant family court commissioner remarked in describing the difference between the role of judge and that of commissioner, "They [the judges] deal with the more lofty issues of the law." (Personal Interview with Commissioner Randall Davis, October 12, 1984.)

Accompanying the formal power which the judge holds are the accouterments of that power. The judicial robes are worn only by the judge, not the commissioner; adjoining each courtroom are the chambers, the judge's private office where discussions with attorneys often take place. In each courtroom there is the bailiff, a sheriff's deputy who maintains order in the court and who at times may be called upon to deal with any verbal or physical altercation which may occur. There is one deputy sheriff assigned to the large waiting area adjoining the commissioner's office. Each commissioner has an alarm button underneath his/her desk to alert the deputy that there is trouble, and that he is needed. A clerk in each courtroom plays an important role in processing the cases which appear before the judge and, in essence, assisting the judge to make wise use of limited time resources. Clerks are not assigned to commissioners; scheduling of their cases is done out of a central administrative office. Face-to-face verbal interchanges are the key elements of the judicial process. Formal, verbal interchanges among participants in the courtroom are recorded by the court reporter; court reporters are not assigned to commissioners. The power of the judge is enhanced not only by the physical decorum of the courtroom but also by the presence of personnel to maintain order, assist in the processing of cases, and transcribe verbal interactions.

This does not mean to imply that only formal interactions characterize all that takes place in the courtroom. Discussions between attorneys take place; attorneys discuss scheduling changes with the clerk while a case is being heard; a phone rings and the bailiff answers it. However, the presence of the auxiliary personnel mentioned earlier is there to expedite what Maynard (1983: 237) refers to as the judicial encounter, ". . . where involved parties officially dispose of individual cases."

Maynard (1983) studied the social processes involved in plea bargaining in a criminal courtroom. He contended that a neglected feature of the study of people-processing organizations was the analysis of face-to-face interactions. In studying plea bargaining in a high volume court, Maynard found that rapid processing of defendants is made possible by ritual practices sustained by all participants. Focused interactions between judges, prosecutors, public defenders, and defendants are necessary to make the process work. The process itself takes place within an ecological order in which a dominant encounter (e.g., between judge and defendant) and subordinate encounters (in the audience section) take place in defined, physical regions of the courtroom.

Although both the family court and the criminal court can be considered people-processing organizations, there are substantive differences between them. Since plea bargaining has become a central feature of the criminal court, it is necessary, as both Sudnow (1965) and Maynard (1983) point out, that a complex set of interactional processes is created and sustained by judge, prosecutor, and public defender. The defendant, of course, becomes a part of this process. Plea bargaining is not a part of family law; therefore, one would suspect that the need for face-to-face interactions among family court professionals, such as judge, commissioner, and social worker would be less than among professionals in a criminal court setting.

This is indeed the case. Judge Alexander summed it up when he said, "We [judges] have little contact with family court commissioners and social workers." (Personal Interview with Judge George Alexander, October 5, 1984.)

The primary area where there is interaction between the judge and another professional is in custody studies. A judge may ask the social worker who did the custody study to be present at the hearing; some social workers routinely appear. Most often reports are submitted to the judge with no in-person appearance on the part of the social worker. The commissioner, however, does exert indirect influence on the judicial encounter. He is responsible for all prejudgment orders, and the guidelines which he sets down under which the divorcing couple must live (matters as child custody and support) often become incorporated as the conditions of the divorce decree.

In the judicial encounters which take place in the family court there is minimal and infrequent interaction between the judge and other family court professionals. Although professionals within the court may not significantly influence the judicial encounter, the role of judge is shaped by both litigants and professionals outside the family court.

The typology presented in Chapter Three (p. 44) is used as a framework by means of which data regarding judges is presented. Internal-personal accounts refer to judges' dealings with litigants whereas external-personal accounts refer to judges' dealings with another element of the judicial encounter—lawyers. Internal-organizational accounts refer to judges' accounts regarding the family court as an organization *per se* and social workers and commissioners within it. External-organizational accounts refer to organizations which impact upon the work of professionals at the court. Internal-ideological accounts deal with how a particular world view on the part of certain individuals or groups shapes the work of the court, and external-ideological accounts deal with how value systems of the broader society and culture shape professionals' work.

The aim of presenting this data is to make clear the work of family court judges and the social structure within which this work takes place, as articulated by one segment of its formal members.

Internal-Personal Accounts

These accounts deal with litigants, who along with judges and attorneys are actors in the judicial encounter. While this first section deals with general statements about litigants, following there are more specific statements regarding litigants.

What does a family court judge do? Susan Samson, the Chief Family Court judge, responds as follows:

> I take a series of statutes on which my authority is based and interpret these statutes in every case that comes before me. The law here is constantly changing. You're riding the crest of the wave of change taking place in our society—nobody can deny there's a cultural phenomenon of living together, it's a recognized way of life—we see what happens when that impacts on the divorce law. This is the court that sees what people are doing in the world. . . It's really interesting. . . It's very exciting for me . . . you have the ability to influence to a limited extent the law. (Personal Interview with Judge Susan Samson, September 21, 1984.)

As has already been alluded to and as will be seen more explicitly later, judges see themselves at times as routine people-processors. However, in the above account the judge sees herself not as a routine people-processor, but as performing the exciting and demanding task of dealing with what happens when cultural forces, brought about by changing life styles, impact on the divorce law. Discrepancies between changing cultural forms and changing statutes which are trying to keep pace, are rooted in this account of people which has both internal (people seen in court) and external (those outside of court) components. People and the way they live, and the changes this entails in family law explains the exciting role of judge portrayed here—"riding the crest of the wave of change taking place in our society."

This account, with references to people, gives some "sense" to the work of the judge. In her role, she bridges the gap between what is happening in the world in terms of how people live and the changing divorce law. The judge's role within the court bridges the discrepancy between these two phenomena. However, as pointed out in the history of the court, discussions about litigants often take on the character of a purely numerical account. By this is meant that judges' accounts of people refer to them as "numbers." An account like this serves to explain that the judge is doing his/her share of work as a people-processor. Judge Robert Reilly (Personal Interview, October 18, 1984) indicated that when he first came to the family court, he had 3,000 pending cases, but that had been reduced to its current level of 1,200. Judge Alexander showed me the monthly report which indicates the number of cases handled by circuit judges. He noted, "I'm doing my share." (Personal Interview with Judge George Alexander, October 5, 1984.)

Litigants as Individuals. Another type of internal-personal account deals with persons who are involved in what I earlier described as the judicial encounter. For example,

> You have to do a lot of explaining to people. This is a high volume court. It's set up to deal with people with brevity. I feel I have a duty to explain things. This slows me down. . . In the area of child support, they're wiped out when they discover they have to pay 17 percent of their income for child support. . . In the trenches they believe they won't have to pay. (Personal Interview with Judge Samson, September 21, 1984.)

Here reasons are put forth as to why people cannot be routinely processed—the fact that people need to have things explained to them validates the role of judge as educator and guide, not merely as people-processor. The organizational discrepancy between people-processing, on the one hand, and attention to the individual case in terms of substantive attention, on the other, is bridged by the judge exercising discretion and determining which case needs greater attention.

Judges use discretion in determining which issues need clarification. In those cases where an attorney has done a good job of preparing his clients for what will occur, little explanation is needed on the part of the judge. However, with the increasing numbers of persons who are not represented by counsel, the judge may feel an obligation to clarify for the involved parties relevant aspects of the law. For example, a couple, not represented by counsel, appeared before Judge Robert Reilly on October 18, 1984. As I observed the proceeding, the judge reviewed the financial arrangements which the couple proposed. The judge pored over the papers for about five minutes, indicating to the couple that he wanted to see if there was any alternative financial arrangement which might be more beneficial to them. This can be viewed as an internal-personal account in which the particular circumstances of the litigants in the judicial encounter permit the judge to exercise discretion and serve the role of a helpful guide.

Another example of a similar account is the following. Judge Alexander states:

> Where there's a marriage of long standing I ask if he has somebody waiting in the wings. If he says no, I talk with them about a legal separation. In this case, the woman can still be carried on her husband's health insurance. I explain to them that with a legal separation there's not remarriage for the next year . . . but the beautiful thing about a legal separation is that you may be able to reconcile. (Personal Interview with Judge George Alexander, October 5, 1984.)

It is worthy to note that on the same day indicated above I was observing in Judge Alexander's courtroom, a couple in their mid-fifties appeared before him. The marriage was of long standing; the husband was employed and had health insurance whereas she did not. Judge Alexander conferred with both attorneys and the couple; he suggested a legal separation because of the health insurance benefit and the couple agreed to this.

Processing Litigants. While the accounts regarding persons involved in a distinct set of circumstances permit the judge to act in a discretionary manner, allowing him to be more than just a people-processor, other accounts reveal that the judge can be no more than a people-processor. "It's gotten to the point where the computer can give the divorce." (Personal Interview with Judge George Alexander, October 5, 1984.)

Judge Lawrence Carroll indicated that because people are no longer interested in reconciliation, the judge simply "rubber stamps" what people want. People's lack of interest as expressed in this account, legitimizes the judges' current role.

> In the old days people would file for divorce and then talk their problems out. We were more of a conciliation court. Because of the no-fault divorce, a judge's decision to grant a divorce is little more than a rubber stamp. (*The Milwaukee Journal,* September 27, 1984.)

Handling Litigants' Emotions. Judges' involvement with people in the judicial encounter also refers to the importance of the litigants' emotional make-up in courtroom proceedings. Judge Samson indicates:

> I saw people crying from relief, from sadness; I didn't see violence in the criminal court. Here you just don't know what people are going to do. I'm a real stickler for control—I'm afraid of emotional volatility—I keep things on a formal basis. (Personal Interview with Judge Susan Samson September 21, 1984.)

Here emotional volatility on the part of litigants is used as justification for a courtroom which is well-controlled, which may make it easier for the judge to carry on her work.

However, changing organizational demands make the management of emotions difficult, as the following illustrates:

> It appears to me that when an intimate relationship is broken up some kind of catharsis needs to occur—traditionally we did it by someone getting in the witness stand and calling him an SOB—then it shifted to money matters—now we're splitting the estate in half. Now it's shifting to custody. I see this necessity to ventilate, but now we don't have much time. (Personal Interview with Judge Lawrence Carroll, Jr., September 24, 1984.)

Expressed here is the need for people to give an assessment in terms of what went wrong in the marriage. However, because of time constraints in the court and a different legal philosophy (no-fault as compared with fault divorce), these explanations cannot occur. It is suggested that people are expressing their feelings in other areas as money matters and custody. The judge in his role in the contemporary court controls the handling of emotions since organizational needs for efficiency require it.

In summary, internal-personal accounts by judges deal primarily with litigants within the judicial encounter. People, at times, are simply viewed as numbers, and the processing of these people legitimates the role of judge as people processor. However, by using personal accounts judges decipher from the routine the particular problem area which cannot be routinely processed. It is to these matters that judges pay special attention. Doing this enables judges to meet the demands of the individual case while keeping the goal of numbers of people processed in mind (Lipsky: 1980). However, being a judge is not only intellectual work, but is also an endeavor in which persons as emotional beings need to be dealt with. Judges' discussions about people and their emotional needs give justification for setting the demeanor of the courtroom. Finally, although judges see people as having emotional needs, because of the prevailing judicial philosophy and time restraints, judges are restricted in terms of their responding to these emotional needs. Most importantly, these accounts about people which see them as "numbers," yet also distinct individuals with emotional needs, provide a basis by which judges can deal with the organizational dilemma of processing people and meeting quotas on the one hand and responding in some ways to their needs as individuals on the other.

External-Personal Accounts

Previously the phenomenon of the judicial encounter was discussed. One actor in this encounter is, of course, the judge; another actor is the litigant. Judges' internal-personal accounts which center on litigants have just been discussed. The third actor in the encounter is the lawyer; judges' external-personal accounts deal with attorneys.

The lawyer is, in a sense, a gatekeeper to the court (Jacob: 1973). To the litigant who is unfamiliar with legal procedures, the attorney is invaluable in assisting the litigant to have his best day in court. The attorney's familiarity with the law and legal proceedings coupled with his knowledge of his clients' circumstances, which he represents to the court in the best possible light, makes him the sole possessor of knowledge of two worlds—that of the client and that of the court.

Although statistics are not available, increasing numbers of litigants in the family court are not represented by counsel. For example, in Milwaukee, "Women Pro Se, Inc." and "Men's Group" educate persons on how to prepare and file papers and represent themselves in their own divorce actions. In spite of this phenomenon, many litigants continue to be represented by counsel. In fact, in the family court, as in other courts, probate, for example, certain lawyers specialize in specific aspects of law. In the Family Court of Milwaukee County, there are lawyers who routinely appear there, having made family law their specialty.

Types of Lawyers and Organizational Work. The types of lawyers which appear in the family court have an impact on the organizational work of judges, as the following illustrates.

> As compared with the criminal law, the spectrum of family court lawyers is broader—it has a good appreciation for human nature—amateur psychiatrist and then at the other end of the spectrum there's some who can't find the courthouse. At times the court has to help the people in spite of their lawyers. (Personal Interview with Judge Susan Samson, September 21, 1984.)

Indicated here is the fact that the spectrum of competence as represented by family court lawyers is problematic to judges. One can surmise that incompetent lawyers make the judges' job more difficult; in fact, the judge may have to spend time helping persons because of the incompetence of the lawyer. This may not only contribute to work-related stress for the judge but also slow the pace of work, affecting the number of cases processed. Thus the judge uses lawyer incompetence to explain some of the difficulties in serving his/her role in the court.

Another similar view of litigants indicates that those who know what is going to happen are easier for the judge to handle. Implied is that lawyers are helpful in assisting litigants know what will take place; however, a problem arises when lawyers, for whatever reason, don't prepare litigants. "The ones [litigants] who understand what is going to happen tend to move more smoothly through the system. There are many lawyers who make matters more difficult." (Personal Interview with Judge Lawrence Carroll, Jr., September 21, 1984.)

Lawyers and Judges' Power. Organizational work for judges is easier if lawyers prepare clients to understand what will happen to them in court. Therefore, as will be pointed out, judges play an active role to get lawyers to make organizational work proceed more smoothly.

From the above accounts it may appear that to a large extent judges are dependent on lawyers for the smooth processing of cases. This is somewhat the case but not entirely so. For in addition to the formal power which the judge exercises over the lawyer in the courtroom (based largely on rules of legal procedure), judges also formulate administrative rules for the courtroom which lawyers are expected to follow. Judge Samson indicated to me that she, Judge Reilly, and Judge Carroll meet often with each other to discuss various problem areas in their respective courtrooms. Some of these discussions center on administrative procedures for lawyers to follow, to improve the general functioning of the family court (Personal Interview with Judge Susan Samson, September 21, 1984). Although I was not an observer at these meetings, they can be viewed as a discussion of accounts by judges regarding lawyers. From this discussion sometimes suggested changes arise for procedures for lawyers in the court; these changes are published in *The Daily Reporter,* the official newspaper of Milwaukee County.

However, the power which judges exert over lawyers is not limited to formal rule changes. In dealing with individual cases, judges may exert their power over the attorneys involved to expedite matters. In the following it is clear that the explanation for some matters moving slowly in court is the behavior of the lawyer.

"After six to eight months if a case hasn't moved, I make the lawyers appear. Too many times lawyers don't want to prepare for a pre-trial." (Personal Interview with Judge Robert Reilly, October 18, 1984.)

Lawyers are key actors in the judicial encounter, and judges' external-personal accounts center on interactions with attorneys. By their competence and behavior lawyers can either make judges' work move more smoothly or impede it. Judges have considerable power over attorneys and can make administrative rules which lawyers must follow in the courtroom. This is done either by an individual judge or when judges meet together, give a series of accounts about lawyers, and prepare changes.

Based on the above, judges see lawyers, because of incompetence and time delays, as impeding the smooth flow of organizational work. However, judges have some active control in promoting greater rationality and adherence to the judges' view of matters by determining the administrative guidelines under which lawyers are to function.

Internal-Organizational Accounts

Judges' accounts of the family court as a formal organization and how it functions are sparse. This contrasts with the accounts of the court, particularly of the 1960's, which were examined in Chapter Two. Those accounts of the court saw it as a legal-therapeutic enterprise which would help heal fractured family life through reconciliation. Some still expect the court to be this kind of healer but this is no longer possible, as the following illustrates.

> Another problem has been created by the courts themselves. In the 1960's, for example, the judge was to see truth and righteousness—I can't do that anymore. In the 1960's there were fewer cases, more time to spend, more resources, and the body of law had remained fairly stagnant. Now there's some dissatisfaction—what they want me to do—retribution for example, I can't do . . . I think a lot of people see the court as a caretaker system . . . I have 1400 pending cases. (Personal Interview with Judge Susan Samson, September 21, 1984.)

Here a variety of organizational variables are presented which shape the role of the judge. For example, in the 1960's, it is claimed that there were fewer cases, more time, more resources and a relatively stagnant body of family law. As a result the judge was revered as the possessor of truth and righteousness. This has changed, and along with it, the role of the judge, although some persons still expect retribution and a "caretaker attitude" from the court. However, organizational demands cast the judge into a role characterized by efficiency.

Judges and Fellow Professionals. In contrast to few references to the family court as a formal organization, there were more internal-organizational accounts with specific references to actors within the organization, such as family court commissioners and social workers. Judges portrayed these persons in different ways, as either assisting them or hindering them in their work. However, the bulk of judges' work is done independently from commissioners and social workers.

This pattern of work affiliation among professionals in the family court contrasts with work patterns in the criminal courts. In a three city study (Chicago, Baltimore, and Detroit) Eisenstein and Jacob (1977) found that prosecutor, public defender, and judge worked closely with each other in the processing of criminal cases. One description of working with others in the court is as follows. Characteristics of a certain professional group, their competence and also their experiences within the court as an organization (e.g. political problems) explain whether or not they can be worked with. In light of this, the following is revealing.

> The system is not set up for judges to interact with each other, but we judges see each other a lot—Carroll, Reilly, and I. I also try to have some idea what goes on in the family court commissioner's office. I think there's a pretty decent rapport between the commissioners and us. Some of the new commissioners are excellent lawyers. I'm impressed with their decisions and what they do. But there are different talents among the social workers—sometimes I get their reports the day the case comes in. The social workers have had political ups and downs and are probably underfunded. I suspect their morale is bad. In addition, they're not well respected by the bar. . . I see their reports, and I've learned not to rely on them. (Personal Interview with Judge Susan Samson, September 21, 1984.)

The above indicates that the primary reference group for the judges is each other, not a work group. This reference group is set up outside of the formal structure; contacts with commissioners are viewed as collegial. While relationships with fellow judges and commissioners are not problematic for judges in their organizational work, this is not the case with social workers. A variety of reasons are presented to show that social workers are difficult to deal with—poor morale, political problems, lack of respect by the bar, and variation in individual competence. However, the chief reason seems to be hastily prepared, poor reports. As a result of this, the organizational role of judge as decision-maker in such matters as custody is impeded.

Judges in their work rely on information gathered by others as a basis for making a decision. Yet judges exercise discretion in terms of how this information is used, as the following illustrates.

> The evaluations are helpful—they're MSW's, and I don't give their reports as much credence as psychologist's and they're overworked. But they do give me a feel for what the children want. (Personal Interview with Judge Robert Reilly, October 18, 1984.)

While information about children is useful for the judge to have, the work of social workers is tinged with some suspicion since, in the opinion of some judges, social workers' credentials are not as sound as those of psychologists. This type of account serves as a justification for the judge to use his discretion in determining what material of the social worker he will use in arriving at decisions about troubles of litigants.

In summary, accounts of the family court as a formal organization are sparse. The fact that the court as an organization has changed (in terms of such factors as larger case loads, less time, and unclear goals) explains in part the altered role of the judge. By far the greatest number of organizational accounts about the family court refers to the roles of commissioners and social workers, and how they assist or hinder judges in their work roles. Judges are complimentary toward commissioners; however, judges view working with social workers as being problematic because of factors as shortage of staff, individual differences in capabilities, and morale problems as a staff. Using such items as a rational pretext, the judge can carefully use discretion in determining to what degree information from social workers will be used in doing organizational work.

External-Organizational Accounts

Judges also explain their work by means of conditions external to the organization proper. In the following, contemporary organizations are seen as being non-supportive for persons in the throes of family conflict. This has had an impact on the work of judges in the court.

> Years ago we denied divorces and people were scared of not getting a divorce. We had a sifting process—pastor, rabbis, and parents said, "Don't get a divorce." We're creating a society composed of people afraid of making permanent commitments—the court isn't equipped to deal with this . . . years ago there were structures to deal with this—

churches. (Personal Interview with Judge Lawrence Carroll, September 21, 1984.)

The above makes clear that professional work in the court reflects a changing moral order. The court no longer actively attempts to preserve marriages but rather makes divorce easier by removing impediments to family break-up. The judge is no longer a potential reconcilor but actually in his role, a facilitator of divorce.

The Legislature and Its Influence. Judges view the legislature as being the single most influential organization in shaping the judicial role, as the following illustrates:

> The use of the word "shall" on the part of the legislature undermines judicial discretion. We have to use discretion. I have to weigh factors or else I invite reversals. . . The legislature is trying to give judges as little discretion as possible. The legislature and public believe that judges abuse discretion as reflected at times in inadequate child support awards." (Personal Interview with Judge Robert Reilly, October 18, 1984.)

Here the judge explains that problems at the court arise when an organization (like the legislature), which does not understand the work environment of the court, acts to control the work of professionals. The culprit is the legislature which dictates the judge's role to such an extent, that all discretion in decision-making is removed. Organizational problems in the form of reversals arise, which can impede the efficiency of the court. The bind for the judge is that he must use discretion to prevent high levels of reversal, yet the legislature prevents this by allowing no options when the word "shall" is used.

Another reason for difficulties in judges' work is to be found in the fact that the legislature, a potential ally, is seen primarily as a detached group, representing a range of special interests, as the following indicates:

> Legislators today in comparison with those years ago are professional legislators; they don't tend to be bankers, farmers, etc., but are beholden to special interest groups. Legislators aren't aware of some of the problems facing the court; for years no legislator has come to talk to me about the problems of the court. Legislators live in a "legislative cocoon." (Personal Interview with Judge Lawrence Carroll, September 21, 1984.)

Implied here is that the court's difficulties, as seen by the judge, are simply not a subject of concern to legislators, even though judges would seem to welcome their interest in the organization. Alluded to in this account is the experience of alienation in the judges' work; he is removed from those forces (the legislature) which could understand the problems of the court and have some power to do something about it.

In summary, external-organizational accounts are sparse in number. However, the accounts given indicate that organizations as the legislature, though having a powerful impact upon the court, do not really understand the work of the court, according to the judges. In addition, those organizations which in the past acted as barriers to persuade persons from obtaining a divorce action no longer serve that purpose. In these accounts judges affirm the need for judicial discretion in order to accomplish organizational work; barriers to this are found in the very organization which passes laws which provide the basis for judges' work.

Internal-Ideological Accounts

Prior to 1936, American sociology was only dimly aware of the concept of ideology. In 1936 Karl Mannheim, German sociologist and philosopher, produced a seminal work on the sociology of knowledge—*Ideology and Utopia.* In this work Mannheim made clear that no human thought, with the exception of mathematics and parts of the natural sciences, is immune to the ideological influences of its social context. Essentially, what ideology states is that knowledge with the aforementioned exceptions is shaped by the specific social interests of participants in a given social situation.

It has been shown in the history of the family court discussed in Chapter Two that ideological accounts are nothing new. An example of an internal-ideological account is that the court should be a court of reconciliation and that in order to accomplish this goal the legal and social work professions need to work together closely. This philosophy was promulgated by those who viewed a major function of the court as that of reconciliation. Other judges did not accept this and put forth the viewpoint that the problems facing the court were due to questionable administrative practices and a general lack of productivity in processing cases. An ideology based on the importance of productivity was espoused.

The most well-known ideological account of the court in the past was the view that the court should be one of reconciliation. It has been shown that due to the impact of no-fault divorce, reconciliation is no longer the primary ideology, but the focus has become one of assisting individuals to calculate the impact of the law upon their personal difficulties—an educational role for the judge. A different ideology in the court entails a different organizational role for the judge as the following illustrates.

> I feel very strongly that our court system could give people knowledge and information about custody and custody awards that courts make. We've been working on developing some kind of movie. People have questions on how property is divided, how child custody is determined, why the court system is so complicated, when is my divorce final, and when can I get remarried? . . .There is a group of lawyers who feel that judges should keep their noses out of it, that it would put lawyers out of business. I don't think that's the case . . . there'll always be a need for lawyers in the family court. (Personal Interview with Judge Susan Samson, September 21, 1984.)

While there is nothing in the above which portrays the judge as a reconcilor, the judge does play an important role in assisting persons to deal with the technical complexity of the court. It is a portrayal of how personal difficulties are organizationally managed by the judge, although lawyers also are involved in that role.

Career Cases. In addition to people who routinely move through the court there is also a group of persons who have continued contact with the court. They have been processed and educated regarding the law, but problems remain; the ongoing reappearance of these persons in the organization results in the expenditure of time and resources. In addition, as the following indicates, the judge does not really know how she, in her role, can assist these persons in dealing with their problems.

> We should have more services for these "career" cases, like counseling. These cases really don't have to do with money, they just haven't settled their differences—they have an active, negative relationship with each other. I don't think that by my divorcing people I can keep them from harm. I don't know what you can do as a court system other than to educate—to push them in the right direction. (Personal Interview with Judge Susan Samson, September 21, 1984.)

Here the judge explains that by dealing with these "career" cases simply from a legal/educational approach, problems for both the persons involved and also for the organization persist. A counseling ideology which would help persons see these troubles as intra-psychic and interpersonal in nature is proposed for dealing with these "career" cases. The organizational work which the judge is proposing is a redefinition of problems, removing them from her jurisdiction and applying a therapeutic ideology.

Judges' organizational roles in the court have changed, one reason for this being the different ideological perspective which prevails in the contemporary court. No longer does the attempt to assist people to reconcile prevail; rather, as has been repeatedly stressed, the court has become a people-processing organization. The emphasis is on an educational ideology in which the judge's organizational role has become one of educating persons about the complexity of the law and its impact on their lives. For people who continue to have repeated contact with the court, judges, in their organizational role, simply don't know how to respond. Attempts are then made to redefine the problem—it is an interpersonal or intrapsychic one requiring therapy, not legal intervention.

External-Ideological Accounts

External-ideological accounts by judges take two forms. One is the breakdown of commitment to traditional family values; the second is the lack of discipline found in American society as evidenced by the people appearing in court. Certainly there is variation among the judges on just how widespread the lack of commitment and discipline are, but one judge, Judge Alexander, sees the breakdown of discipline as explaining all of society's problems and the difficulties of people who appear in the family court.

The Breakdown of Commitment. In the view of one judge, the lack of commitment to family values on the part of people has made it difficult to know how to respond to this phenomenon. A certain helplessness in the role of the judge can be implied from the following.

> The concept of commitment is so devoid in our society. People are afraid of commitments to family values. The court isn't equipped to deal with this; years ago there were structures." (Personal Interview with Judge Lawrence Carroll, September 21, 1984.)

While in the past institutions such as churches assisted persons to deal with problems of commitment, this is largely no longer the case. The lack of commitment to a relationship is seen as a reason for persons appearing in court. Implied in the above description of the judge's organizational work role is the desire to be of assistance, but this is not possible since the necessary prerequisite—commitment—on the part of persons appearing in court is absent.

Earlier in this chapter a statement made by Judge Samson regarding what she described as "a cultural phenomenon of living together" was discussed. This phenomenon was referred to by all the judges, thus indicating that it no doubt has an impact upon their work. It certainly indicates a shift in values, away from traditional family ones, perhaps toward more individualistic ones. This ideological shift has also had an impact on judges' organizational work.

Organizational work, as a result of the impact of living together upon the divorce law, has become more complex for judges in terms of their need to spend more time educating people as to what the law means for them.

The Breakdown of Discipline. While three of the judges give few external-ideological explanations for their organizational work, Judge Alexander, in stark contrast, sees all of society's ills as due to the conflict between lack of discipline as acted out by forces in our society and other, more traditional values. It is usually a battle between those who espouse love of country, duty, and commitment to traditional family values and those who do not. Here is a sampling of some of Alexander's viewpoints.

> Women became liberated and thus destroyed the family unit. . . Within the last twenty years there's been a breakdown or lack of discipline in our schools. In the Korean War there was a complete breakdown of the American fighting man—it was the first time in war that no American prisoner tried to escape—it was a breakdown of discipline. . . A lack of discipline has destroyed the family—people who can't discipline themselves are getting married.

Alexander asked rhetorically:

> What will save the country? The answer, that every man will serve—some kind of compulsory military training. But not women—they're special—they have a great burden—to bear and raise children. (Personal Interview with Judge George Alexander, October 5, 1984.)

What impact do these ideological viewpoints have on the judge's organizational work? Judge Alexander states, "We deal with the failures here—the people who wanted an easy way. . . It's gotten to the point where the computer can give the divorce."

Alexander also contrasts the criminal and the family court and indicates that, "In the family court the judge can be a hero, you can give the people what they want; in the criminal court you can't give them anything." (Personal Interview with Judge George Alexander, October 5, 1984.)

Here ideological accounts are used to explain the routine nature of organizational work, so routine that a computer can do it. The reason for this, according to this view, is that all the people in family court are failures who lack discipline and want an easy way out. In his role at the family court the judge is an ambivalent hero—legitimator of what people want but also in his role of divorce grantor he sanctions what he terms the "lack of discipline."

External-ideological accounts refer to matters as discipline and commitment and their breakdown in contemporary society; most of these explanations are not elaborate. The exception is Judge Alexander's accounts which are powerful, though value-laden explanations for organizational work and the functioning of the court generally.

Summary

It has been shown that a variety of explanations are presented by judges to deal with organizational discrepancies and also legitimate their own work role. If judges are viewed as street-level bureaucrats one of whose primary functions is that of people-processing, one would expect accounts regarding people with whom judges directly deal to be most frequent. This is the case. Accounts regarding those involved in the judicial encounter—litigants and attorneys—are most frequent, followed by those of organizational actors—commissioners and social workers—who sometimes aid and at other times hinder judges in their work. Judges view organizations, as the state legislature, to be basically non-supportive of their work and also see a breakdown of traditional structures, as churches, which in the past dissuaded people from divorce. Ideological viewpoints of the judges deal with a perennial organizational dilemma—processing functions versus quality services to the individual. Judges call for more education regarding the law for people; education frequently takes place in court and adds to the judge's organizational work. Ideological forces in terms of lack of commitment and discipline is given in some accounts, but only Judge Alexander sees ideological accounts as having a major impact upon organizational work.

In summary, the judges' major work is to process people efficiently while at the same time trying to educate and zealously guard the importance of judicial discretion. Their work is done pretty much alone, without commissioners and social workers, but lawyers must be dealt with constantly. They see organizations as being non-supportive of their work; this is occurring against the back-drop of ideological forces which erode commitment and discipline. Judges' support of each other in peer groups deals with issues confronting them and ways to handle it (especially lawyers) and perhaps the work seems less lonely as a result.

CHAPTER FIVE

SOCIAL WORKERS AND WHAT THEY DO

A Departmental History

IN CHAPTER TWO a history of the Family Court of Milwaukee was presented. As was pointed out, because of their power and influence, judges have played a key role in the history of the organization. In addition, the Family Court Commissioner and Family Court Counseling Services also have exerted some influence upon the court's practices and procedures.

Certainly the influence of Family Court Counseling Services, where social workers are employed, is less than that which the judges have historically exerted. However, before accounting practices *per se* are discussed, in the following pages the history of this department and its influence upon the court are considered in some detail. As will again be discussed later, the history of an organization, in retrospective debates among members and others concerned, provides a series of accounts for existing conditions of various kinds. The department's history enters into accounting practices in two ways. First, as was discussed in Chapter Three, accounts provide a stock of knowledge which organizational members can use to explain, justify, or excuse work practices and thus create rationality. The second way is that the replacement of the director of the department is illustrative of problems encountered in administration in a street-level bureaucracy, which in turn affects work practices of service providers. This will be discussed in greater detail later.

Despite the fact that a counseling department has existed within the Family Court of Milwaukee County for fifty years, relatively little is known about its inner workings. If names have significance, it is relevant to note that in 1935 the department was called the Domestic Conciliation Department. By 1962 the word "family" replaced domestic and the department was called the Department of Family Conciliation. In 1982, the conciliation function was de-emphasized and the department became known as Family Court Counseling Services.

In Chapter Two it was noted that much of what is known about the Milwaukee family court is based on newspaper reports. In the 1960's the socio-legal court with its emphasis on reconciliation and the rights of children in divorce was the focus. Differing judicial viewpoints centering on these issues were discussed. In these newspaper reports, issues and personalities became entangled; specifics, as numbers of cases processed, frequently became a part of these discussions.

In the 1980's the professionals of the family court who were the target of investigative reporting were the family court commissioners. In 1982 (August 16-20) *The Milwaukee Journal* published a five-part series on the work of the commissioners, examining not only their work practices, but rationales for various case decisions, along with their use of work time. More recently, both *The Milwaukee Journal* and *Milwaukee Sentinel* investigated the work of the family court commissioners. The reporting centered on the operation of this office, individual commissioners, use of their time, and the Chief Family Court Commissioner's supposed lack of control over his staff. The upshot of the reporting was an audit of the department along with recommendations for reduction of staff and monitoring of the commissioner's work schedules (*The Milwaukee Journal,* April 4, 1985; *Milwaukee Sentinel,* April 2, 1985).

Family Court Counseling Services and its work was never subjected to as much public scrutiny as either the work of the judges or the commissioners. The primary reason for this seems to be the fact that in their capacity at the family court, social workers are relatively powerless in terms of decision-making ability. For example, in two matters where social workers spend the majority of their time—custody investigations and mediation of visitation—the social worker makes only recommendations to the court and the court hands down a legal decision.

However, the work of the then Department of Family Conciliation was criticized in a story in *The Milwaukee Journal* (June 9, 1976). The focus of criticism was on the work of the department in the conduct of group sessions to fulfill the mandatory one session requirement for couples contemplating divorce. As will be recalled, the Wisconsin Family Code of 1969 required that at least one party in a divorce action meet a one session counseling requirement. In Milwaukee County because of the large number of persons processed in family court, group sessions have been held for a number of years. For example, in 1975, 7,000 persons attended group meetings (*The Milwaukee Journal,* June 9, 1976) conducted by social workers of the Department of Family Conciliation. These meetings were criticized in the article mentioned above because, if the focus was to be reconciliation, this could not be successful if only one person in the action was expected to participate. However, the director of the department from 1971-1982, Charles Grover, defended the counseling sessions as helping people think about their situation and enabling them to achieve more successful problem solving.

In the article just referred to, the counseling sessions were not the only item criticized. Judge Raymond Podell, a family court judge, criticized the custody reports of the social workers as inadequate. Prior to that, in open court, he indicated that one reason he requested a transfer from the family court was because of difficulties in working with the Department of Family Conciliation. Grover replied that the problem was due to staff shortages in spite of the fact that the staff consisted of fifteen full-time social workers. Dissent in the department appeared to focus on Grover. Herman Lowell, a social work supervisor, retired two years earlier than he had orginally planned. He gave sixteen hours notice and quit because, "I couldn't take Grover anymore. . . Grover centers on how people dress, and makes sure they come to work at 8:00 instead of 8:03. But he's completely devoid of giving any leadership to the department." (*The Milwaukee Journal,* June 9, 1976.)

Yet disenchantment with Grover was not limited to members of the department; lawyers became concerned about the rapid turnover among social workers, and what they perceived as the poor quality of their work (*The Milwaukee Journal,* June 9, 1976). Grover tended to ignore this criticism, believing that the department was generally doing a good job. He did admit, however, that more cases seen in the department could have been referred to other community agencies, thus lessening the need for additional staff. (Personal Interview with Charles Grover, December 5, 1984.) However, sentiment against Grover continued to build among judges and lawyers in the community. Pressure placed upon County Executive William O'Donnell and the Finance Committee of the Milwaukee County Board of Supervisors led to decisive action to restructure the department. Eight positions were eliminated, Grover was dismissed, and only six MSW social work positions remained. The Director of the Family Reconciliation Department, who had reported to the Chief Family Court Judge, now reported to the Chief Family Court Commissioner, thus tending to weaken the influence of the director upon the presiding family court judge.

Bob Frances, a veteran of the Milwaukee County Civil Service System and for eleven years prior to coming to family court, a social worker at the Milwaukee County Children's Court, was appointed as the Chief Social Worker at the family court in August, 1982. The six MSW social workers who served under Grover remained on.

When he first came to the court, Frances indicated that he:

> . . . couldn't figure out what the goals of social work were here. Now I see this as a child welfare agency. Our goal is to put kids in the best possible post-divorce situation and see that they have as much contact with both parents. Most of the time marriage counseling is done for the benefit of the children. In mediation you're neutral, sit back . . . they make the decision. I'm not sure that that decision is in the best interest of the children. (Personal Interview with Bob Frances, November 28, 1984.)

Frances also convinced his superior, Family Court Commissioner Michael Phillips, that the social workers would accept only court-referred cases. Prior to this, it was routinely assumed that social workers would automatically deal with such problems as visitation. Accepting only court-referred cases limited the number of cases active in the department.

Frances also reassured his staff that they would be treated as professionals. He told them that he would not harass them on cases so long as quality service was being provided. Frances indicated:

> I wanted to remove the dictatorial control which workers felt under Grover. He forbade his workers to talk with judges and commissioners on a one-to-one basis. He had special padlocks installed on filing cabinets . . . the man was paranoid . . . he was a snoop. (Personal Interview with Bob Francis, June 6, 1984.)

Frances points to the fact that under Grover's regime grievances were filed by union members at the rate of two per week, but since Frances has been there no grievances had been filed, and morale among the staff had improved.

As noted in Chapter Two, the history of an organization can be viewed as a series of events which appear in different accounts seen from different perspectives. While accounts serve to explain, justify, or excuse organizational behaviors since they are also put forth by actors with differing viewpoints, they also take the form of competing rationalities. This is quite evident in the debates between Grover and his detractors with each side advancing accounts for that which it did. What is most relevant for the discussion at hand is that on the basis of the Grover incident, it appears that power in a street-level bureaucracy is not maintained by being a "good bureaucrat"—strictly adhering to detail and operating on the basis of a hierarchal authority within a department. Rather, one factor for success seems to lie in maintaining flexible working relationships with others and recognizing a person's need for autonomy.

Current Family Counseling Services

Today, Family Court Counseling Services is located on the seventh floor of the Milwaukee County Courthouse. Next to these offices are the offices of the Family Court Commissioner, Deputy Commissioner, and Assistant Commissioners. Two family courtrooms are across the hall. A receptionist and several clerical personnel round out the staff of six social workers and chief social worker. The offices of the social workers are small, about nine feet by twelve feet, and only two have windows. They are all brightly lit with fluorescent lights, have desks usually heaped with papers, several armchairs for clients, and posters with optimistic nostrums are characteristic wall decorations.

The work of the department centers on the provision of individual and group counseling and the conducting of custody and mediation studies. Contact with clients can be as short as one interview or one phone call. For persons who have continued contact with the court system, contact can extend over long periods of time, with welfare of children receiving major attention.

In the following section of this chapter, social workers' accounts of their work are presented. As a guiding framework, the typology presented in Chapter Three is used. As will be pointed out, social workers' accounting practices—the prevalence of varied types of accounts—depend on the condition of their work, especially with whom they are working at the time an account is offered. Group versus individual work affects accounting practice such that accounts in groups explain how parts of the organization work. As social workers describe this, group members learn what impact organizational practices may have on their personal difficulties. Whether this knowledge will assist the client to deal more effectively with the organization is an open question since many circumstances along the course of the client's journey through the organization will affect the final outcome. As will be explained later, individual work is different.

Accounts in Group Work

The primary work of judges, commissioners, and social workers at the court involves services to individuals. However, of these three professions, only social workers are involved in the provision of the services to groups. I have already discussed that a provision of the Wisconsin Family Code of 1960 was mandatory counseling, of one session, for at least one party in a divorce action. Because of the large number of persons processed in the court, this counseling has typically been provided in groups. For example, in 1975, more than 7,000 persons were seen in group sessions by members of the Department of Family Conciliation (*The Milwaukee Journal,* June 9, 1976). Typically, two hour-long sessions are held each week. One session is for persons with children; another session is for persons without children. The average attendance is about 18-25 persons, and the group is conducted by one social worker. Proof of attendance at a meeting is needed to obtain a court date; persons can also fulfill the mandatory counseling requirement by obtaining counseling from a therapist, minister, or priest in the community.

The meetings themselves are conducted in a relatively small, narrow room which has a low ceiling and which seemed somewhat cramped for the thirty people in attendance when I observed at the meeting. At the front of the room where the social worker stood were a table, chalkboard, and hanging plants. A poster with two adults and a child and the words, "My Tomorrows Depend on Your Love" was on a wall. Behind that was a window overlooking another part of the courthouse.

Accounts, as noted in Chapter Three, are one way of explaining personal difficulties; they are identified, reacted to, elaborated on, and in some cases transformed into a particular type of deviance. These processes center on efforts to do something about the presenting problem and are critically shaped by the nature and direction of the intervention of an outside, usually official party (in this case, the helpful professional). The form which a problem assumes is a product of micropolitical struggles for the legitimation of official organizational agents (Emerson and Messinger, 1983). I have indicated that accounts can be viewed as the means whereby problems are elaborated and given meaning. Following the typology, the locus of accounts can be found in people, in organizations, or in ideology.

By participation in a group, the individual acknowledges that his/her personal difficulty has become a public matter. Although the nature of the problem probably will not be discussed in the group, the fact that in the act of being there, the participant meets a requirement to obtain a court date means that the problem is taken seriously. The presence of an official party, the social worker, legitimates the official nature of the process (Emerson and Messinger, 1983). Although the formal purpose of these groups is still reconciliation, when the social worker in the several groups which I observed asked how many were there for conciliation, not a single hand was raised. What then is the purpose of these groups? They can best be understood as a process of anticipatory socialization in which participants are given clues as to how the organization handles problems—shaping and forming them and in some cases defining them as deviance; at times suggesting official action on the part of the court's agents, such as denial of visitation. As mentioned earlier, group participants are given hints as to how problems are handled by the organization when social workers present accounts about agents of the court such as judges, or reveal some of the workings of the organization through explanations stressing time lines leading to the final divorce hearing. Finally, ideological accounts stressing individual problem solving and rationalization are presented to participants to assist them bridge the gap between life before and after divorce.

Internal-Personal Accounts. In this study, internal-personal accounts deal with accounts regarding litigants in a legal action. Note the form this type of account takes as a social worker talks before a group of individuals who have children.

> Going through a divorce, people feel down on themselves. It's a rough time! You may not have enough money to get things. Pick up some books you like to help you. This is a good book [refers to the book in front of her]—*The Boys and Girls' Book About Divorce.* It may help you to answer some questions you have about divorce and explain this to your kids. Often parents want to stay together for the children's sake, but if you have parents griping with each other, we have found sometimes that children's grades actually go up after a divorce. If you do have hostility towards your spouse, talk to a therapist, a minister, or friend, but don't talk to your child about your spouse. If your [support] check is late in coming, don't say to your child, "Your dad never sends the check on time or your mom doesn't send the money"—it works both ways. (Observation at Group Session conducted by Betty Tucker, February 9, 1983.)

Here the focus of attention is the person and his/her children living through divorce. Actually it is a series of accounts which the social worker has culled based on her experience in working with others. It is anticipatory socialization for the divorce experience itself. In this presentation divorce is pictured as being difficult, but manageable, if explained openly to children and if hostility doesn't reach deviant proportions. (It is suggested that hostility be managed through therapy.) An ideology of management of emotions through use of a third party, a therapist, is also presented. For the social worker, the presentation of this account validates the official view that problems are handled through individual management—awareness of one's emotions and willingness to seek therapy, if necessary.

External-Personal Accounts. Other internal-personal accounts characteristically contain the elements presented above. External-personal accounts, on the other hand, those dealing with persons such as attorneys who are part of the judicial encounter but are not part of the family court organization, are sparse. The form which such an account takes is as follows. The social worker explains the legal, time sequence of divorce.

> We start with the filing of papers. Let's call the point, "A." There are a lot of things to be taken care of before you reach point "B"—this is appearing before the judge. Your attorney can help you. (Observation of Group Session conducted by Marge Brown, February 10, 1983.)

This rational description of the court, focusing on the attorney, views him as assisting the client to presumably take care of the items necessary to obtain a divorce. In his role of gatekeeper at the court (Jacob, 1973) the attorney assists in expediting the handling of problems so that the desired goal can be obtained. It is also implied in the above account that the social worker in her organizational role is a part of this sequential process and presumably works to achieve rationality.

Organizational Accounts. Organizational accounts presented in the group are primarily internal in nature, that is, they refer to the court as an organization. The only external-organizational account presented in the group involves a reference to a program at the Milwaukee Area Technical College, which was founded several years ago to assist homemakers who had been out of the work force for a number of years to return to work. This program was mentioned at a group session as being of use to persons who had been at home for a number of years and now contemplated return to work. This account explains how an organization can assist in redefining a personal difficulty and help create a new role—a member of the workforce. It legitimates the social worker's role as one who is knowledgeable about problem management.

However, the majority of organizational accounts are internal in nature, dealing with the court. These accounts are of two types—one type of account explains elements of the organizational structure of the court; the second type provides information about the organization. The following is an example of how the organization works. A social worker states:

> A pretrial takes place in the chambers of the judge—it's not an official hearing—it's a checkup period. You can tell if it's going to be a contested divorce—then you're placed on the contested calendar. If everything is worked out in terms of stipulation, you are put on a default calendar. I would recommend being put on a default calendar. A contested divorce can take a long time. We see a lot of them when there are custody issues. The longest one that I remember is a family where a custody fight went on for three years. A default hearing, on the other hand, is very simple. (Observation of Group Session conducted by Marge Brown, February 10, 1983.)

In presenting information on how the organization processes cases, clients are encouraged to handle their problems in such a way that movement through the organization is simplified. In socializing clients to the ways of the organization, the work of the bureaucrat and level of activity in problem management may be reduced.

Another type of account provides simple information about the organization.

> *Mrs. Smith:* "Does visitation have to be scheduled through the courts?"
>
> *Social Worker:* "No. But if one party feels that they are not getting enough visitation, they could contact our department and we would set up the schedule." (Group Session Observation conducted by Betty Tucker, February 9, 1983.)

This is an example of how the organization handles one type of problem—visitation. The dispute is taken out of the hands of the differing parties and the official third party intervenes, settling matters in one way or another. In the matter of visitation as with most family court matters, problems are not intrinsic to a relationship, but extrinsic, requiring third party intervention (Emerson and Messinger, 1977: 126).

These views of the organization presented to clients explain how the organization works and in particular how discrepancies are dealt with. These accounts are compilations of the street-level bureaucrats' ongoing experience within the organization—a view to which the client does not have access (Lipsky: 1980). However, by listening to these accounts, the perceptive client can learn how the organization handles certain kinds of problems. Sometimes the client can even learn to avoid the organizational intrusion into his life by handling his own affairs as much as possible.

Internal-Ideological Accounts. In Chapter Two it was indicated that the most common particular, internal-ideological account of the court in the 1960's under Judge Hansen had been the view that the court should be a court of reconciliation. Today not only do professionals at the court not present this view but even clients do not see the court as one of reconciliation. In fact, groups are still supposed to focus on reconciliation (according to state statute), but both leaders and participants know this will not take place. As a social worker stated at the opening of a group session,

> A main reason for this counseling is to see if reconciliation is possible. My question to you at this time is this, and I want you to think about it before you raise your hand. Is there anyone here who came for help in reconciliation? (The social worker smiles as no hands are raised.) Is there anyone here who had doubts regarding divorce, some question whether you want to go ahead? (Again, there is no show of hands.) Usually I get at least one hand that goes up . . . well, most people do want to go ahead with the divorce at this time. (Observation of Group Session conducted by Marge Brown, February 10, 1983.)

Here reconciliation is not a solution to the family problems which clients have. Agreement on the part of both group leader and participants that reconciliation is not a solution gives the street-level bureaucrat the ability to explain other avenues for dealing with problems. The account validates the social worker role of non-reconcilor of marriages.

External-Ideological Accounts. These accounts deal with the impact of external ideological factors upon organizational work. The ideology presented stresses individual management of problems by means of looking at the difficulty in a rational manner. If this fails, intervention by a third party, in this case the social worker, provides therapeutic assistance.

Here a social worker presents a divorce as a rational process, capable of management by the individual without organizational intervention.

> I'm going to talk about the stages you go through in divorce. The first is denial—you deny what is happening. Then depression, then anger—your spouse, you think, could have prevented the divorce. Then bargaining, and if you can't make an agreement, then you hope you can move on to divorce and accept it. There are losses, but there are gains. If your spouse argued at dinner, now you can enjoy mealtime. But there will be changes. Happiness can be a gain—getting out of a bad marriage. Divorce now doesn't penalize you—anyone can get a mortgage even if divorced. Anything you've wanted—you can still look forward to getting it. (Group Session Observation conducted by Betty Tucker, February 9, 1983.)

The above conveys the belief that divorce as a problem is manageable by viewing it as a linear process with distinct psychological phases. Divorce is no obstacle to happiness; the ideology stressed is individual awareness and management. The underlying message may be, "Handle the aftermath of divorce yourself."

Another account is as follows:

> How many of you have noticed that because of divorce your friends are acting differently toward you? You may have to start to make new relationships; there's "Parents Without Partners" and Catholic family groups. Go into these groups where there are people restructuring their lives like you. (Observation at Group Session conducted by Betty Tucker, February 9, 1983.)

Here is stressed the individual's responsibility to expand his/her identity through affiliation with groups. It is another model for the handling of troubles; a shared identity can arise through the recognition of mutual problems.

These ideological accounts, presented by organizational troubleshooters, offer contemporary wisdom regarding the management of divorce. The role of the street-level bureaucrat is to offer this as advice; it is incumbent upon the individual to make use of it and to thus manage his/her problems.

For most persons, attendance at a group session is their first encounter with the family court. By their attendance it is acknowledged that a personal difficulty or problem has become public; the presence of a street-level bureaucrat, a third party, legitimates this (Gulliver, P.H., 1969: 11-23). The presentation of accounts serves to explain how people are managed and organizational practices occur. Management of divorce based on ideological viewpoints is also present although how one's particular problems will be handled is not clear since a large part of the management of problems is based on circumstance and discretion, based on rationales the street-level bureaucrat alone has access to (Lipsky, 1980; Emerson and Messinger, 1977).

Finally, in the presentation of accounts to clients in these groups, a rationalized picture of problem management is presented. Dealing with organizational discrepancies is the task of the street-level bureaucrat and not privy to clients. However, the rationalization of problems is the task of street-level bureaucrats and clients alike and some procedures for achieving this are shared in the group.

Accounts in Working with Individuals

When social workers in individual work are considered, accounting practices shift from an emphasis on socializing clients regarding organizational problem management to dealing with individual cases. In dealing with individuals, their personal difficulties are scrutinized and "packaged" to the extent that service providers can deal with these cases and eventually discharge them from the bureaucracy. The amount of contact which the individual has with a service provider varies widely. For example, judges may hear a trial in which support and custody are hotly contested matters. In contrast, a default divorce with no support or custody issues involved may take only a few minutes.

Individuals with whom social workers have contact usually are involved in matters of custody and visitation. Very often children and what is in their best interest becomes a focal point of attention. In the matters to which social workers pay attention, three areas stand out. First, they are investigators who gather factual information for judges and commissioners. Second, they make recommendations regarding what is in the best interest of children of divorcing couples to judges and commissioners. Judges and commissioners act upon these recommendations and then make decisions; social workers have no formal decision-making power at the court. Third, social workers are involved on a first hand basis in dealing with the problems that people bring to the court, assisting them within the broad context of organizational demands of a people-processing court. Many times these difficulties are presented in the form of a crisis, which tax the social workers' analytical and management skills.

In Chapter Four "the judges' court" was discussed. There is also a "social workers' court" and the following accounts, illustrative of how problems are handled, will now be discussed.

Internal-Personal Accounts. Most of what social workers do involves individual contact with clients; the following account is typical of how a social worker sees her work at the court in relation to individuals.

> Family Court Counseling Services used to have a horrible reputation—people came to us thinking it would be a waste of time. It's better, but we lost staff—we really need two or three more counselors. The caseload gets tremendous. Burnout is here—there's never a good case. There's a family, children breaking up—anxiety and frustration—the longer you're here the more overwhelmed you become. It's a good job though; there's some satisfaction in helping some people. I'd like us to do more counseling and mediating rather than investigating.

> If we could show them there's a more constructive way to end things rather than what we do—investigating. Then there's the element of surprise—35 percent of our time is spent in dealing with phone calls about immediate problems as visitation, kids not going to school. (Personal Interview with Marge Brown, September 27, 1984.)

The nature of difficulties which social workers face at the court is explained as being partially due to the social-psychological state which people are in due to family disruption. As will be recalled, judges made similar statements about difficulties in dealing with people who are encountering social-psychological problems. However, problems presented do not follow a routine course and about a third of the social worker's job involves dealing with the unpredictable presentation of difficulties. This account also contains references to the organizational context of handling problems. The organization is short-staffed and the emphasis on investigation rather than counseling and mediation does not help families handle their difficulties more effectively. The view of burnout presented here as having its roots in the interaction between the organization and service provider confirms Karger's (1981) view of burnout not as an intrapsychic phenomenon but as related primarily to the structure of work within which service providers find themselves.

The above account portrays individual, personal difficulties presented to the social worker as being problematic to manage and almost impossible to resolve. The emphasis is on the pathology of the client—problems are seen as intrinsic to the client. This contrasts with the view of organizational work presented earlier in "Accounts in Group Work" where intrinsic factors are explained as being non-problematic if clients are knowledgeable about organizational procedures. In spite of the difficulties which clients present and organizational constraints, legitimation of the helping role is found in "some satisfaction in helping some people."

Information gathering. One of the primary tasks of the social worker is to gather information regarding matters of custody and visitation so that the judge or commissioner has more factual material on which to base a decision. While this appears to be a relatively simple procedure of interviewing family members and those knowledgeable about the family, it is a procedure beset with difficulty. One put it this way:

> Social workers are effective only if they can establish rapport with their clients. That in reality is their chief resource. At the same time, we have to respond to the court to help them make decisions. The information given to the court is information taken from the clients. If they

> trust us, they will give us the information. This middle role is difficult for us to maintain. We do this in custody and visitation matters where we work with both clients. I try to work so that if I make a decision in favor of one party, that I let the other party know that I did what I thought was best, but I still want to maintain a working relationship with the party against whom I made the decision. If the decision goes against somebody, they may feel animosity. One way I have of handling this is that before a custody recommendation, I get both parties in about a week before and tell them why I have made a certain recommendation. (Personal Interview with Ted Christiansen, March 2, 1983.)

The above clarifies the fact that in order for the social worker to obtain information the role must be explained as being non-adversarial. Persons are seen as being capable of animosity if the information-gathering process is not handled delicately. Related to this is the fact that the handling of problems at the court by social workers is often not a simple open and shut matter. For example, one social worker estimated that in a number of cases, ongoing problems need to be dealt with.

> About 35 percent of our time is spent in working with phone calls about visitation, kids not going to school—immediate crises. (Personal Interview with Marge Brown, September 27, 1984.)

Crisis and case management. In the following, reference is made to the crisis nature of some of the social worker's job.

> Forty percent of the work is crisis work. To the people it's a crisis . . . but not for me. Because after you receive four to five calls a day like this. . . I think on some occasions they could solve it. (Personal Interview with Keith Norwich, September 28, 1984.)

A problem is defined differently depending on how and by whom the individual case is evaluated in comparison with the overall "stream of cases" (Emerson, 1983: 426). For example, Bloor (1976) found that parents and doctors evaluate children's symptoms differently. What parents see as exceptional and unique, the specialist sees an another instance of a routine case encountered in the course of his work. As such, accounts for the "same" problems vary and cannot be understood separately from the context of interpretation.

Yet management of problems is a key element of the social worker's job.

> We get all the complaints. . . Judge Carroll tells people, "If there are any problems take them to the social worker." Like the call that interrupted our interview (during the interview we had been interrupted by a phone call)—there's been alcoholism, sexual abuse, kidnapping of

> children, mother took the kids to New Mexico . . . all that was dumped on me. Sometimes you feel you're being trampled on. (Personal Interview with Marge Brown, September 27, 1984.)

This account states that an official role for the social worker is that of "organizational problem manager." The explanation for this is the fact that people at times present complex difficulties that the legal appointees of the court simply can't handle in the form presented.

In contrast to the judge to whom matters are presented in an organized fashion, difficulties are often presented to the social worker in a rather disorganized way. The social worker serves the organizational role of organizing these problems and presenting them to the judge in a coherent fashion.

Social workers as persuaders. Although social workers assist the court in the management of problems, the means of doing this are a lot less forceful than those available to a judge or commissioner who can issue legal orders. Social workers, in contrast, rely exclusively on rational problem solving, persuasion, and consensus between parties to make problems more manageable. For example,

> It's in parents' and our interests to get people to agree. If I can get them to agree—I don't have to keep dealing with that case. I like the fact that we use persuasion. Some people say, "I really don't want to go back to the judge or commissioner." (Personal Interview with Betty Tucker, September 26, 1984.)

This, then, legitimates the role of the social worker's use of persuasion for several reasons. First, people favor it because if agreement is not reached a formal appearance before judge or commissioner takes place. Second, it is in the social worker's own interest to persuade people to agree, for otherwise, additional attention to the case is needed. Third, getting people to agree makes future court appearances unnecessary, relieving a burdened court system.

However, internal-personal accounts about clients frequently refer to the fact that because of the nature of clients' difficulties, rational problem solving cannot be used. For example,

> I'd like to get them earlier to do something with their lives. Reasonable people go to agencies to get help with their marriages. However, we see some very unreasonable people here. For example, I know a father who is a homosexual, and his wife is very upset about his visitations with the child. I have been trying to convince her that she is being somewhat unreasonable. After all he is not a pedophile. (Personal Interview with Bob Frances, February 14, 1983.)

An effort here is made to manage problems, in the form of conflict about visitation, in a rational manner. However, rational management is not successful because the mother is seen as being unreasonable; social workers offered many similar case examples. The battery of therapeutic tools did not work because people were seen as being unreasonable and presenting their difficulties in a way that was not amenable to rational management. Failure or lack of success in this instance is considered to have no organizational basis. Rather, it is explained in terms of the client's intrinsic resistance to the reasonable alternative presented to her.

These internal-personal accounts just discussed illustrate that problem management in which social workers are engaged is complicated by the fact that frequently problems are presented to them in an unpredictable, disorganized fashion by persons who at times are unwilling to respond to what social workers believe to be rational approaches to problem solving. Even information gathering is considered to be a source of difficulty since the social worker believes in the need for an ongoing relationship for future work. However, the reality is that his recommendation for custody, for example, will favor one party and not the other. These accounts illustrate that the dilemmas of the social worker within the court are interpreted as being due in part to the unpredictability in which persons present their concerns, the unreasonableness at times of people with whom social workers deal, and the problem of trying to maintain a working relationship with two opposing parties. While the role of the social worker at the court espouses information gathering and rational problem solving, accounts about clients explain why this role is so problematic.

External-Personal Accounts. External-personal accounts concern problems stemming from those persons outside of the formal family court organization with whom social workers have contact. Attorneys and mental health professionals, as psychologists and psychiatrists, constitute this group.

Although social workers indicate that they are able to maintain working relationships with attorneys, for the most part, this has not always been the case. One social worker stated the following: "Mr. Phillips [the Family Court Commissioner] used to call Family Court Counseling Services the dumping grounds for attorneys." (Personal Interview with Joanne Randall, September 28, 1984.) This statement was corroborated by another social worker.

> There used to be a lot of sending people to us when attorneys could have settled it . . . in the past lawyers dumped on us. When we started to charge fees in 1982 we changed the attitude of attorneys. (Personal Interview with Bill Schwartz, September 20, 1984.)

The reluctance of attorneys to have their clients incur additional expense has led to a more discriminating use of social work services. In addition, the recent emphasis on court ordered referrals for matters of custody and mediation, and then case closure after services, has led to a more structured, less open-ended approach to service provision.

Although this arrangement has tended to make the social worker's job a bit easier, problems remain. Reasons for this are rooted within the organization and the individual attorney.

> If we had more time, we could talk with attorneys to tell them what our work really is. You have some attorneys that beat you over the head, figuratively. The more adequate attorneys can take disagreement." (Personal Interview with Bill Schwartz, March 7, 1983.)

Here the social worker indicates that a problem in terms of establishing working relationships with attorneys is due to the fact that the time demands incurred by organizational factors simply do not permit the social worker to clarify his role. In addition, the statement contains a reference to individual differences, intrinsic factors, among attorneys that make work with them problematic. This indeed is the case since a wide range of attorneys practice at the court—from family law specialists to those who have a general law practice and appear there infrequently. Both judges and social workers agree that the wide range of attorneys who practice at the court is problematic. However, while social workers have little ability to control attorneys' actions in court, judges, as was discussed in Chapter Four (p. 55), can do so by requiring attorneys to adhere to certain administrative rules in the courtroom.

Social workers' problems with power. These accounts center on social workers' limited power within the organization and their efforts to deal with this in the course of their organizational work.

At times social workers and attorneys appear to vie with one another regarding how to assist a client in resolving problems. The social worker sees himself/herself as emphasizing openness between him and the client, resolving difficulties, and working through conflicts. In the following account a social worker indicates that the social worker's view of problem resolution is impossible to implement due to the "advocate attorney's willingness to simply get the client what he wants."

> Sometimes in a case, attorneys are a big factor but the most serious problem is the advocate attorney who represents any position which the client asks for; it's impossible to penetrate that. . . It's an alliance between attorney and client that can't be opened. The worst is when a stipulation is established and nothing has been worked through; the attorneys simply get together and write up something. I think the attorneys believe it will work but they don't want to be aware of all the person's distress. (Personal Interview with Bill Schwartz, October 4, 1984.)

In the above, the social worker's involvement in the handling of problems is simply precluded by an alliance between attorney and client. Such a justification for non-intervention serves to absolve the social worker from performing an organizational role since the lawyer-client alliance makes social work intervention impossible. However, "advocate attorneys" at the court seem in the minority. Another account stresses mutual cooperation in the management of difficulties between attorney and social worker making it possible for the social worker, in particular, to fulfill his/her role.

> We get a tremendous amount of support from the legal community. Even the attorneys are not our adversaries by and large. Most want to settle these things and not fight them to the death. (Personal Interview with Paul Miller, March 3, 1984.)

While positive working relationships between social workers and lawyers have just been referred to, attorneys' powerful roles as representatives of clients along with their ability to present arguments in court, places social workers at a decided disadvantage.

> There's a lot of politics involved. There's a scouting report on us. Some attorneys have wealthy clients—they follow a certain procedure. The only thing we have going for us is rapport—make each client feel comfortable in telling you the truth. When the social worker goes to court, he has no one to back him. (Personal Interview with Ted Christiansen, September 28, 1984.)

Here reasons are given why social workers are less powerful than lawyers. Social workers are "used" by attorneys, by means of political maneuvering. In addition, it is implied that for social workers, "rapport building," is based on creating an atmosphere of openness; however, attorneys' tactics are different. Finally, in the legal arena of the courtroom, the social worker is isolated because of his/her less powerful legal role as compared with that of the attorney. This account implies that structural factors, which give more power to the attorney, explain the more limited power of the social worker and the subsequent problems involved in performing his/her role.

In addition to attorneys, social workers also have contact with mental health professionals such as psychologists and psychiatrists. As was discussed in Chapter Four, (p. 58) some judges are more apt to put more credence in the opinion of an M.D. (psychiatrist) or Ph.D. (psychologist) rather than a master's degree social worker. As such, social workers often feel locked into an information gathering role and are intimidated by more prestigious professionals. Venturing outside of that role is difficult as the following comments illustrate.

> You recognize that the people with power will always win. You have to stick as close as possible to your information gathering—you can't argue before a judge or commissioner. You're a social worker—you use observation. I felt in an unusual position in February. Four psychiatrists testified. If I didn't go, I would receive a subpoena, the attorney said. In writing up my opinion I had to view the psychiatrists' opinions and parents' opinions. I know I wasn't supposed to say anything against the psychiatrist—I worked at a mental health center years ago. Here at court there's my idea of a judge or commissioner. He says, "I can't get any idea of what it is like in their home; I want somebody with some smarts to gather information." The weakness is that the social worker doesn't have an equal position with the guardian ad litem. I argued against the claim of a psychiatrist that the father had a serious problem and needed treatment. I argued that he had a serious illness, but he worked—he had an M.A. and worked full time. I supported the father. I reviewed the social history of the father, not focusing on his internal state of mind—then I was thinking about those four psychiatrists—I took the position that the father could have custody. The court accepted it. I was asked a few questions from the opposing side. I don't want many cases like that in my lifetime. Essentially in most cases we're not expert witnesses—we're in the gray areas of being an expert witness. (Personal Interview with Bill Schwartz, September 20, 1984.)

The above is illustrative of the process whereby the social worker's version of problems and suggestion for management is presented in court. The focus is not on the internal state of mind of the client but rather on social facts. The viewpoint of the social worker is legitimated by the court supporting his version of the client's difficulties. In spite of the social worker's fear that his version may not be accepted by the court, the psychiatrist's version of the individual's difficulties are explained away by the social worker. The above comment also illustrates that for a variety of reasons, sometimes the less powerful win in court.

In summary, external-personal accounts address social workers' relationships with attorneys and mental health professionals. Although working relationships are established, certain types of attorneys ("advocate attorneys") make social work management of client problems extremely difficult. Since social workers are powerless to argue in court, unlike attorneys, their chief tool is to divert client problems from the court system and try to assist them in the counseling arena. Unlike judges who possess power to manage attorneys' presentation of material in the courtroom, social workers simply cannot do this. A final account in this section dealt with social workers' relationships with other mental health professionals. It is illustrative of the fact that credentialism, though powerful, is not as powerful as judicial discretion in decision making.

Internal-Organizational Accounts. As mentioned earlier in this chapter, each social worker except one, who had no experience in the prior administration, made references to organizational life under the former department head. Accounts about the old regime are instructive since they reveal that some ingredients of bureaucratic failure are considered to be.

> Our director had been our supervisor, but when he became a director, he "processed" us—I mean, he used what he had told us as a supervisor, but now he had the power of director behind him. He would tell us to do something and we wouldn't do it, and then he became irate. He would make unreasonable demands of people, and would insist on things like women not wearing slacks to work. Finally, the administration got him out in the name of budget cuts. (Personal Interview with Bill Schwartz, March 7, 1983.)

These comments reveal that following what traditionally is thought of as traits of bureaucracy—strict adherence to rules and obedience to one's superior—is actually dysfunctional in a street-level bureaucracy as the family court. Another problem in people-processing organizations which the above touches on is how administrators in such an organization obtain information about what workers actually do. This problem is one of compliance observability and Prottas (1979: 145) indicates that it is a perennial problem for police organizations and street-level bureaucracies generally. In the account above, the supervisor had information about workers' activities and compliance with rules. However, when the same supervisor became director, he used this information along with the increased power of his office to demand compliance. The response was a negative one, the workers zealously guarding their autonomy to function in a manner which they felt reasonable, not responding to what they considered to be "unreasonable demands." The account makes clear that differing rationalities existed in the same department in this bureaucracy until "order" was restored by redefining the problem as an economic one.

In a second historical account about the organization, two administrations and their differing impact on worker performance are discussed.

> There has been substantial improvement in the current administration of the social work department. When you compare the two administrators, in the current one there's more independence for the workers. There's more opportunity to do a creative job, and we're not as hampered now by excessive rules and regulations. We can decide how to divide up our time each day and do what is most important. (Personal Interview with Betty Tucker, March 1, 1983.)

As was just discussed, ineffective employee performance is ascribed to functioning under "excessive rules and regulations"—a commonplace view of bureaucracy. Here the opportunity to perform creative work is linked to being independent and having discretion to decide what aspects of one's job are important. Employee effectiveness is related to the presence of autonomy and discretion and inversely related to excessive rules and regulations.

Contemporary organizational accounts. While workers say they cherish autonomy and link competence with the ability to exercise discretion in what they do, other accounts about the organization clearly indicate that autonomy of social workers is limited. This is due to a number of factors. First, social workers find themselves in a legal setting where the legal profession and its ability to advance a legal world view are strong. Second, judges and family court commissioners are simply more powerful—they are the decision makers at the court. Third, time factors and especially unpredictability in terms of how social workers become involved in cases tend to decrease autonomy. In addition to historical accounts about the organization, other organizational accounts center on the organization *per se* and its impact on social workers' roles, other organizational participants as judges and commissioners, and extraneous factors such as time, which shape worker performance.

One account which deals with the organization *per se* addresses the issue of having the necessary information to do one's work.

> The organization itself, you wonder how much it's changed. Three years ago, three-quarters of the department was laid off. They still have the judges and the family court commissioners in the same spots. The clerical mess is still the same—you have no idea how irritating that

is. In a critical case I have, I got a scribbled note on a little piece of paper from paternity. [One family court commissioner hears paternity matters.] When paternity doesn't give you histories, you're functioning in limbo. We have a huge problem in working with other agencies and courts. It's really an information/retrieval systems problem . . . here you are saying "yes" to your client about visitation and the most recent stipulation may not say that at all. . . I have to run around getting the information I need—in this one case, the paternity order wasn't written up. (Personal Interview with Joanne Randall, September 28, 1984.)

While workers in interviews complained about the demands of paperwork in their jobs, the above reveals that simply obtaining knowledge of what is happening in other parts of the organization is problematic. Not knowing how other persons in the organization have handled client problems can cause the social worker to manage them differently. Implied in the account is the desire on the part of the social worker to efficiently do her job, but an organizational-wide problem of communication makes this difficult. The social worker makes do and scurries around for the necessary information.

While the sharing of information within the organization may be problematic, interpersonal communication among professionals at the family court reveals struggles related to status, trust, and autonomy.

Some people on the staff feel there should be closer contact with family court commissioners and judges. I've heard some family court commissioners say they won't read our report until after a decision has been made. . . The distance they seemed to keep from us to be more objective is not a problem for me. . . It's nice when you can talk with someone in the hierarchy—corporal talking to the general—there is that feeling. That's part of the legal system—they do use negative reinforcement as their *modus operandi*—the attorneys get it too, you know. The advantage of not having much to do with them is that there's more autonomy; we can work with our clients as we see fit. (Personal Interview with Joanne Randall, September 28, 1984.)

Here interpersonal communication is problematic because of status differences in the organization. But even more than that, communication does not enhance one's work. In response to negative experiences of dealing with legal professionals, an organization niche characterized by autonomy is available. The social worker's solace becomes work with clients who are not enmeshed in the legal system.

The social worker's role in the court is illustrated in the following:

I guess part of it is knowing that some cases we can deter from the legal system—some cases that come to us for study for custody—I work with them. Some of these families I can help to avoid the legal system. These are the families I enjoy working with—even with visitations to have them come in, to get them to focus on something else—their kids. It's better than those cases where we have to go through heated courtroom battles—these are the real problems. I think some of these problems can be avoided by avoiding the legal system. (Personal Interview with Marge Brown, March 4, 1983.)

This account indicates that social worker satisfaction is seen as increasing with the type of clients seen—clients that can be helped to handle their problems by diverting them from the legal system. A technique which social workers use to accomplish this is to help clients redefine the problem, to see it as a relational issue with children, not solely a spousal issue. Perhaps more importantly, social workers play an important organizational role by assisting individuals in handling problems so that further intervention by the legal system is not necessary. Deviant cases can be viewed as those which become involved in courtroom battles and need extra intervention on the part of professional personnel. These cases are time consuming and exasperating for the court. The following remarks summarize some of these issues.

The courts will always need someone like us, they have to come to decisions quickly; they don't want to hear stressful cases. We help them go ahead—theirs is a rational process; ours is less exact. (Personal Interview with Bill Schwartz, September 20, 1984.)

Thus, the social workers' roles within the organization can be seen as diverting cases from the court if possible, and assisting persons to handle problems before they become defined as deviant. However, as seen earlier, when the court becomes involved in situations where parties cannot agree (custody issues), social workers provide information about the parties which the court can use to reach a decision. The above account characterizes the court as employing a rational decision-making process. Social workers make some of this rationality possible by processing and packaging (preparing) cases for review. The rationality employed by social workers is different from the legal rationality as will be seen in the section on ideological accounts.

Although social workers play an important role in assisting legal professionals process cases in court, this is not a one-sided relationship. The following indicates that commissioners provide support for social workers in their work.

The family court commissioner is our main source of help when problems persist. Any parent who interferes with visitation we refer back to court. Family court commissioners are also tired of seeing the same

> problems exist. I think it's due to the fact that the courts are overloaded, they don't have time to keep looking at the same case. (Personal Interview with Betty Tucker, September 26, 1984.)

Here it is shown that reciprocal, helping relationships between professionals exist at the court. A particular form of problem management (counseling) may be resisted by the client; in that case another form of problem management is introduced—legal intervention. Implied is the view that persuasion is of limited usefulness in people-processing organizations where a more forceful mode, such as the power of the law, often gets quicker results.

A final internal-organizational account deals with the organization's limited resources to accomplish tasks; in particular the lack of time which social workers have to do their job. Lipsky (1980) has provided extensive documentation that street-level bureaucracies have limited time resources to do work.

> The problem is that we don't have the time. Time is the problem. What I've seen a lot of is burnout—at times each staff member is overburdened—we have no control over our case load—a case can flare up into something big just through a phone call. (Personal Interview with Ted Christiansen, March 2, 1983.)

"Burnout" is seen not as an internal phenomenon but as related to the worker's lack of control over time resources. (See Karger, 1981, for a similar explanation.) It has been said that one of the chief functions of social workers at the court is to deal with those problems which legal-rationality cannot handle. However, this task is made difficult through unpredictable intrusions into the work day of the social worker.

Prottas (1979: 145) has pointed out that all street-level bureaucrats employ techniques to manage allocation of time resources.

> Well, we don't have the time here to do the job—we skim over the surface. Even custody is skimmed over. We're not controlled by our social work instincts but by the way the court sees it, and that is to make a recommendation and stick by it. It does take away the powers of the social worker to provide services. Essentially, we're private investigators. We can't work intensely with the family. We hope someone out there at the agencies picks up the problem. In a sense, we pass the buck. (Personal Interview with Marge Brown, March 4, 1983.)

This account explains two techniques of problem management—skimming and diversion. Skimming is a management technique of service providers. Certain cases, for a variety of reasons, whether because of organizational demands or the personal preference of the service provider, receive full attention while others receive scant attention. Diversion directs persons out the system, unclogging the system but serving the organizational task of husbanding scarce resources. This is done in this instance by referring troubled families to community agencies which presumably have more time to work with them.

The range and richness of internal-organizational accounts just presented indicate that the practice of social work is markedly influenced by the organizational setting in which it occurs. In the case of the family court, social workers' discussions of their work indicate that their making sense of organizational life is a major task for them.

External-Organizational Accounts. Organizations within county government have a significant impact on the operation of Family Court Counseling Services. The County Executive's office was influential in the reorganization of the department several years ago. As a social worker describes it:

> There was quite an impact on our department by the County Executive—they determined two years ago that we didn't need fifteen people in the department here—a community feeling that what we're doing wasn't important. The director wasn't functioning in a significant way. There were two to three union grievances a month. The national news picked up on an order by our director that a secretary here couldn't wear a certain blouse because her navel was exposed. He went around to the judges trying to get an order. The community's idea of what we were doing was influenced by those things. The County Executive picked up that the judges couldn't support family court counseling. Within a six month period, eight people were taken out of their jobs. Our department is back to its role of gathering information when the court is in need. (Personal Interview with Bill Schwartz, September 20, 1984.)

Although the social work positions in the department are civil service ones, the county executive intervened because of the problems which the department's director had created. Apparently the department's reputation for effectiveness had also been tarnished. Implied here is that the functions of the department were reduced by the sharp curtailment of staff. Additionally, it is also hinted that during the cutback, the role of the social worker was different, but has now been restored to gathering information. The account makes clear the dramatic impact of an external organization upon social work functioning.

Of course, for such a striking change to occur, an issue must be present. A social worker describes how an issue is created.

> Organizational changes are related to how things became an issue—it was spoken around court that Grover wasn't doing well. The County

> Executive isn't involved that often—he's involved with budgets but they put pressure on our performance—formulas that they pull out of the administrative hat. (Personal Interview with Bill Schwartz, September 20, 1984.)

As noted earlier (p. 84) people were disenchanted with Grover's close adherence to bureaucratic guidelines; this became an issue which prompted intervention. In the final portion of the above comment, organizations which attempt to monitor worker performance are seen as acting capriciously. The social worker quoted above has his own formula for effectiveness: "The height of effectiveness is when we can keep a case out of court." (Personal Interview with Bill Schwartz, October 4, 1984.)

These accounts are instructive since they indicate that bureaucratic competence as demonstrated by Charles Grover, the former head of Family Court Counseling Services, became dysfunctional with severe consequences for the department. As indicated earlier in this chapter, ingredients for administrative success in a street-level bureaucracy are elusive, and as the above account illustrates (Personal Interview with Bill Schwartz, September 20, 1984), subject to evaluation based on rationalities which may not be compatable with intrinsic problems of street-level bureaucracy.

Internal-Ideological Accounts. Social workers present a wide range of internal-ideological accounts, but no external-ideological accounts, as do judges who see external organizations such as the legislature as making the laws under which judges function and often limiting judicial discretion. Social workers, on the other hand, are less influenced by an external organization, as the legislature, but because of their limited power, more subject to organizational constraints. These internal-ideological accounts deal with ideas and/or world views which influence the way in which social workers go about doing their work.

I have discussed earlier in this chapter that when the current head of Family Court Counseling Services took up his duties in 1982, he was unsure about the goals of the department. The following deals with departmental goals and their changing character.

> When I first came to the court I couldn't figure out what the goals of social work were here. Now I see this as a child welfare agency . . . our goal is to put kids in the best possible post-divorce situation and that they have as much contact with both parents. Most of the time marriage counseling is done for the benefit of the children. . . In mediation you're neutral, sit back . . . they make the decision. . . I'm not sure that that decision is in the best interest of the children. (Personal Interview with Bob Frances, November 28, 1984.)

Currently social workers see themselves as advocates for children, according to this account. It has been shown in organizational accounts that because of social workers' lack of power within the organization that advocacy for children is frequently not possible. However, child welfare advocacy is stated as a primary goal of the social work department in spite of this. Implied is the idea that social workers use persuasion to convince those with power to act for the benefit of the child. It is interesting to note, and not entirely clear why social workers see their major goal as being child advocates when, in cases where the welfare of the child is the major concern, the court appoints a guardian ad litem who has the power to present legal arguments before the court, whereas the social worker does not. It could be argued that guardians ad litem represent only a minority of children involved in divorce and that other children, social workers believe, also need advocacy services. It has also been discussed in Chapter Two that a variety of ideologies have arisen in the family court from time to time. As the above account implies, the latest one on the horizon is mediation with the idea of neutrality and perhaps less use of persuasion. The outlines of a dilemma for social workers are stated in the above—child welfare advocates versus neutral professionals. It is suggested in the above account that guiding ideologies for social workers are subject to change. This is made clear when we examine an account which traces how the family court has changed the way in which it has handled conflicts.

> Prior to 1978 when no-fault came into being, one's day in court was very important therapeutically. But with no-fault there was such a volume that the courts couldn't really listen. No-fault appealed to the courts because it appeared to be cheaper, because less time was involved. No-fault was created by avant-garde people on the assumption that most people could handle their own thing. But the energy to fight was carried to custody battles and visitation. (Personal Interview with Charles Grover, December 5, 1984.)

This suggests that prior to no-fault divorce the courtroom was the battleground where conflicts were resolved. However, because of increased volume due to no-fault divorce, time was not available for prolonged courtroom battles. Also implied are that the problems which people bring to the family court are psychological in nature; that people seek a resolution, and that now the focal points of conflict are custody and visitation. If custody and visitation become the new focal points of conflict and yet courtroom time to manage these is lessened, a major organizational role for social workers emerges—making custody and visitation matters rationally manageable for the decision makers in the court—judges and commissioners.

The difficulties of investigating. However, investigating is not an easy task for the social workers and complicates their role as the following illustrates.

> As an evaluator, you make judgements about them [clients]. It's hard because you just have yourself and your own experience—things that you think are important. In some instances you will find both parents are equally good. . . But essentially the work is all situational. (Personal Interview with Paul Miller, October 12, 1984.)

The problem in performing an evaluation is one of having few normative guidelines to reach a decision; every case becomes a new situation. The reason for this is that empiricism, or gathering of facts, with no explicit framework (although there probably is an implicit one) is the ideology which guides the social worker in his/her role as an investigator. As has been discussed, the empiricists are not the decision makers at the court; the power to interpret the facts rests ultimately with the judges and commissioners.

Conducting investigations is further complicated by the fact that cooperation is necessary from clients but it is not always forthcoming. The following account which contains references to both ideology and clients, explains the difficulties in the social worker's investigative role as due to clients' ideas that supplying information may not be in their best interest.

> Here the goals seem to be—get a report done. I really didn't want to do investigative work. I started by having to learn the court system and what to expect from attorneys and judges. Part of the problem with working here is that sometimes families see us as the enemy—snooping around—investigating—there are a lot of barriers in terms of cooperation. Time it limited in terms of trying to arrange mutual cooperation. (Personal Interview with Marge Brown, March 4, 1983.)

Problems doing therapy. While social workers view investigative work as mundane, they view therapy as a more enterprising endeavor, but something which is difficult to practice, given their role in court.

> Sure, I'd like to have some therapy cases . . . but there's a role conflict—a little therapeutic relationship is formed but then they go to court—it's a fairly tense situation—our information shared in court is based on a relationship. It becomes fairly public. (Personal Interview with Bill Schwartz, September 20, 1984.)

While therapy is viewed as an essentially private encounter between therapist and client, this belief is not accepted by the court which is probably the one arena in our society where information must be shared. Organizational requirements regarding the sharing of information limit the degree to which therapy can be used within the organization.

Although the court may view social workers' doing therapy as problematic, clients are also reluctant to see social workers as therapists.

> We don't get into deep therapeutic relationships with the people in which they share all with us and work through things. I don't think we're into that kind of role with them. They see us as the government inspector—and they try to influence us to side with them . . . that's natural. . . I find a lot of times it's other things that are influencing these people. I don't see myself as being that therapeutic in terms of being professional. (Personal Interview with Paul Miller, March 3, 1983.)

Implicit here is the shared belief by both social worker and client that therapy is not a priority; rather, the goal is for the client to present facts to the social worker in the best possible light. By precluding a therapeutic role, the social work role of information gatherer is legitimated.

Futility at the court. The most frequent type of account of an internal-ideological nature deals with social workers' sense of futility in regard to their work. Here the social worker explains his/her limited effectiveness as a problem manager. The reasons for this are several—the type of persons with which the court deals, the nature of their problems, and the fact that social workers espouse an ideology which sees these difficulties as being irreconcilable.

> I just try to survive it. It's so difficult to know what criteria to focus on—children's rules, who disciplines, how, whether they're stable people or just how much can a single mother or father expect from their kids—all kinds of stuff you have to wade through, and financial, too, of course; who gets the home, all sorts of things and the kids most always are caught right in the middle and everybody wants to find out what the kids think and feel. I believe for the most part parents try their best to be as objective and nonhysterical about their spouse when they talk to the children but there's no getting around that when people enter custody disputes they're downright angry and they still want their position to prevail—they're in a combative mood. (Personal Interview with Paul Miller, October 12, 1984.)

While the above makes reference to people and the difficulty in assisting them to handle their problems in a rational way, especially in matters regarding child custody, what is most problematic for the social worker is the uncertainty of knowing what guidelines or norms to use to evaluate families. Even though custody investigations are a distinct type of case handled within a caseload, and one might expect a systematic approach to these cases, each case is approached on an individual, *ad hoc* basis. Studt (1972: 50-51) in his study of parole agents reports a similar phenomenon. By looking at each case as idiosyncratic, the social worker with each new evaluation, ferrets out what he thinks is relevant information, thus preserving his role to use discretion.

Another account stresses the lack of normative guidelines for social workers to use in their work.

> What you need to do in this job is have a lot of confidence in your own judgments, be assertive. I find the more of these cases I do, the less confidence I have. . . These situations are so complex . . . my feeling is that there is no perfect answer, that everybody loses something. When you get it all over, you really don't know what the truth is anyway. (Personal Interview with Paul Miller, October 12, 1984.)

The above explains away reasons for the ineffectiveness of the social worker. It is to be found in the nature of situations and people with which social workers deal; the lack of normative guidelines for dealing with family breakup makes satisfactory resolution difficult for families to reach.

Effectiveness of social workers is also related to the type of ideology which the court permits them to use to assist clients manage problems.

> There's never a good case—there's a family, children, breaking up, anxiety, frustration—the longer you're here the more overwhelmed you become. I'd like us to do more counseling and mediating rather than do investigating. If we could show them there's a constructive way to end things rather than what we do—investigating. (Personal Interview with Marge Brown, September 27, 1984.)

The types of situations which people present are problematic and the main priority appears to be investigating, not counseling. The ineffectiveness of the social worker is explained by the difficult problems which are presented and the idea of the court that social workers are to spend their time conducting investigations.

A final account makes clear that norms to assist families adjust to post-divorce life are vague.

> It's trying to help people work out their separate lives and help their children without damaging each other, and it means being an ongoing battleground. It's helping children deal with the fact that they'll be in blended families—it's a whole new ballgame for everybody these days. It's going to be harder for them. I don't know. The family court is here, I guess, to resolve these conflicts. (Personal Interview with Paul Miller, March 3, 1983.)

Here the social worker's primary task at the court is stated as investigation; however, according to the above, what is really needed is assistance for persons adjusting to post-divorce situations. But social workers' organizational role is that of fact-gathering, and in this aspect, the ideology of empiricism is the guiding light. Social workers see a real need for counseling persons and assisting them to cope with post-divorce situations. However, as Bohannan and Huckleberry (1968) indicate, when families fail, the court or no one else for that matter, knows how to assist the family to recover, short of remarriage which contains its own set of problems. As a society we simply do not have a set of norms and back-up institutions which assist families to deal with the aftermath of divorce. What is most striking in social workers' ideological accounts is a recognition, on the one hand, of the needs of families to reconstruct their lives following divorce. On the other hand, and this explains the social workers' frustration, they can be of little help to families because of their primary role in the court as investigators. In addition, what is problematic for social workers in counseling situations is the fact that society has not enunciated norms for post-divorce families and therefore the intervention of social workers is limited.

These ideological accounts reveal that the ideas and/or world views which guide the family court as an organization also have a marked influence on what social workers do. While the court casts social workers in the role of information gatherers, social workers are not content to see themselves only in this light and they also try to act as child advocates and mediators. In addition, social workers may wish to see themselves as therapists, but to do therapy in an arena where all information must be shared is difficult. Yet social workers enjoy doing therapy and believe that therapy can be effective and can divert clients from further court contact. The ideology which seems to have the greatest impact on social work functioning is what can be termed the ideology of futility. While social workers may believe that a primary task is to assist families establish meaningful lives after divorce, society does not offer norms and guidelines to achieve this, and thus social workers find the task of helping problematic and at times futile.

Conclusion

In reviewing social workers' organizational work at the court, several points are worth noting. First, social workers view the intrinsic problems of clients as difficult to manage organizationally since these problems are presented in an unpredictable fashion, frequently requiring quick intervention. A chief task of the social workers is to organize these problems into a coherent form so that other professionals at the court can make decisions about them. In contrast to judges who express great concern about the number of cases processed, social workers are less concerned about numbers of cases, but more concerned about time spent in preparing cases for judicial processing or else applying therapeutic interventions so that further judicial processing is unnecessary.

Second, by far the greatest number of accounts presented by social workers deal with how their organizational work life is shaped by their lack of power in the organization. Their powerlessness is evident when they describe their relationships with attorneys who often tell their clients what kind of information they should share with the social worker. In contrast, judges' organizational power is evident in their ability to set administrative guidelines for attorneys' courtroom conduct.

Finally, judges' ideological accounts focus on what they perceive as the breakdown of commitment and loyalty to the family in persons appearing before them. This coupled with no-fault divorce makes it virtually impossible for the judge to play the role of the reconcilor. In a similar manner, social workers espouse what can be termed an ideology of futility, meaning that social workers in their organizational role of problem managers often feel helpless to be of assistance to individuals coping with personal difficulties. A reason for this is that American society does not offer normative guidelines for post-divorce situations. Both judges and social workers experience the futility of organizational work—brief encounters with troubled persons toward whom the application of professional expertise is difficult since both professionals and clients are enmeshed in a social process for which no clear normative guidelines exist.

CHAPTER SIX

FAMILY COURT COMMISSIONERS AND THEIR WORK IN THE COURT

AMONG THE professionals in the court—judges, social workers, and commissioners—the role and function of the commissioner seem to be the most complex. Therefore, prior to discussing the commissioners' own description of their work using the typology of accounts, their role within the court and the setting in which they do their work is discussed in some detail. As social workers and judges have had their work criticized, likewise has criticism fallen on the commissioners. In the final section of this chapter, recent critiques of commissioners' work are presented; such an analysis raises issues of how rationality is maintained but also questioned.

The Commissioner's Role and Function

In contrast to judges and the relatively clear work role which they project to the public, is the role of the commissioners within the court. Certainly the role of the judge has been written about extensively in both the professional and popular literature while relatively little is known about the work of the commissioner. Hansen (1966: 12-14) pointed out that commissioners and referees have been part of the American system of jurisprudence for some time. Commissioners are lawyers by training who are an arm of the court and are able to conduct certain hearings and make certain judgments. For example, in Milwaukee County, court commissioners are assigned to children's court, small claims court, traffic court, misdemeanor court, and paternity, which is actually a division of the family court. In Hansen's (1966) view, the use of commissioners by courts to conduct preliminary hearings, for example, allows judges to concentrate on more substantive issues. Hansen's belief in the importance of commissioners was reiterated by Judge Robert Curley, a former chief family court judge in Milwaukee County, "There absolutely is no way the family courts could function without them [the commissioners]." (*The Milwaukee Journal,* August 19, 1982.)

As will be recalled from Chapter Two (p. 17), the Family Court of Milwaukee County was created by the Family Court Act of 1933 and along with it, the position of Family Court Commissioner. However, it was not until 1961, primarily as an upshot of the Wisconsin Family Code of 1959, that there was a family court commissioner, sometimes with an assistant, in every county of the state. The duties, responsibilities, and powers of the commissioner are clearly spelled out in the state statutes (see Appendix D). Special rules apply to Milwaukee County (probably because of its size) where among other things family court commissioners are classified as civil service positions. Ultimately each commissioner is selected by the chief judge of the judicial administrative district from a list of eligible civil service candidates.

The chief judge not only appoints the commissioners but the work role of the commissioners is also shaped by the chief family court judge. For example, in one county in Wisconsin—Waukesha—commissioners were recently given the power by the judges to grant default divorces (*Milwaukee Sentinel,* June 29, 1984). This is not the case in Milwaukee County, although the chief family court judge there will at times assign specific matters to the commissioners. For example, due to recent statutory changes and upon order of the chief family court judge, commissioners now hear domestic abuse cases and can issue a temporary restraining order.

While commissioners may be assigned additional duties from time to time, the bulk of their tasks remains essentially the same and are as follows. If the parties in a divorce cannot agree to the rules under which they will be living prior to the final judgment of divorce, they must appear before the commissioner for a first hearing. Usually both parties and their attorneys appear at this hearing. At the hearing the commissioner will decide who will receive custody of the children, who will visit the children, and under what circumstances; who pays support and in what amount, who pays what bills, who lives where, and who pays what debts. This is done by means of a temporary order which remains in effect until the judgment of divorce is entered or the case is dismissed. Orders coming out of this initial hearing are quite important since they set the conditions under which the divorcing couple will live prior to their final appearance before the judge for the judgment of divorce. While commissioners play an influential role in determining the conditions under which the couple will live prior to the divorce, they also become involved in enforcing the judges' decrees once the divorce has been granted. For example, if the judge ordered certain custody, visitation, and support arrangements which cannot be followed for a variety of reasons—unemployment, for instance, the commissioner meets with the couple and counsel and tries to work out a suitable alternative.

While part of the commissioner's job involves being a legal-human relations specialist, resolving disputes in matters of custody and visitation, a substantial part of the job deals with the enforcement of support orders. Wallerstein and Kelly (1980) and Cassetty (1978) point out that the enforcement of child support has become a national problem. Although currently there is no comprehensive federal program for enforcing payment of child support, the states have taken the initiative in devising innovative programs for the collection of child support. In Wisconsin, garnishment and wage assignments are routinely used as administrative tools for child support collection. However, under provisions passed by both the Wisconsin State Assembly and Senate in the 1983-85 budget bill, paycheck withholding will become a standard procedure in 1987 for all new child support cases. This procedure can also be applied to all cases that return to the court. Simply put, child support payments will be deducted from one's paycheck. Although not mandatory, percentage-of-income standards are being used to determine the level of child support. For example, for one child, 17 percent of the absent parent's gross income; for two children, 25 percent; for three children, 29 percent; etc., are the guidelines suggested. As will be seen later, judges and commissioners have resisted the imposition of mandatory guidelines, expressing the need for judicial discretion in determining child support levels. In the Family Court of Milwaukee County, the responsibility for the enforcement of child support orders falls upon the commissioners. Their ultimate sanction is to send the individual to circuit court to be dealt with by the judge. This is not usually done and commissioners view support issues as a socio-legal and not strictly as a legal matter.

The important role which commissioners have in the collection of child support monies is most clearly seen in the paternity division of the family court. Commissioners are assigned, on a rotating basis, to serve in this division. Paternity matters deal with the adjudication of alleged fathers and the awarding of support to minor children; Milwaukee County has aggressively pursued obtaining monies from these fathers. In fact, five corporation counsels representing the county and a full-time commissioner have been assigned to this division. The commissioner currently serving in the division commented about the work in paternity matters, "Our main function here is to get money." (Personal Interview with Commissioner Sam Martinez, October 5, 1984.) These strong efforts have paid off and the funds collected as a result of commissioners' hearings have risen dramatically in recent years (see Appendix E).

Commissioners and Their Work Setting

The family court commissioners' offices are located on the seventh floor of the Milwaukee County Courthouse. On one side of that floor are two family judges' courtrooms. On the other side of the hall and to one's right as one gets off the elevators are the offices of Family Court Counseling Services—the social workers. At the other end of the hall are the waiting areas, hearing rooms of the commissioners, and the clerical section which handles secretarial work for the commissioners. The Chief Family Court Commissioner is Michael Phillips, who has held that office since 1978. There is also a Deputy Commissioner, Herbert Steiner. In addition, there are seven full-time assistant commissioners.

One enters the commissioners' office complex by means of a glass door on which are printed in black letters, "Family Court Commissioners." To the right, are listed the names of the current commissioners. As one enters, immediately to one's right is a small office area with several clerical personnel at desks; there is a counter hemming in this area at which persons transact business with the staff. The primary function of the office is to schedule motions for the commissioners, publish the daily calendar listing the motions each commissioner will hear that day, including the times—usually first hearings are given thirty minutes, others fifteen minutes, and register walk-ins—persons who come to the office without an appointment but who need to speak with a commissioner about a matter such as support, custody, or domestic abuse.

In 1983, 22,280 motions were heard by the commissioners ("Statistics, Office of the Family Court Commissioner, 1984"). However, many more motions were scheduled by the office just described. Both Chief Commissioner Phillips and the office estimate that one-third of all scheduled motions "fall off." This is a term used in the commissioner's office to denote motions which are not heard when scheduled; they are settled or adjourned to a later date. A perennial complaint of the office which writes the calendar is that attorneys do not give them enough notice to remove a case ("a take-off") so that another case can be added. Writing the calendar is also complicated by the fact that at times family court commissioners are transferred to serve at children's court or traffic court, sometimes necessitating quick realignments in the calendar. In addition, walk-ins need to be seen—sandwiched in between scheduled hearing times. When I observed at this office on October 12, 1984, the first available hearing date was for December 7. Of course if an individual protests by stating, "I can't wait that long," the secretary at the desk suggests that she/he talks with the chief or deputy commissioner, who will listen and might tell the secretary, "Put it on someone's calendar." (Personal Interview with Pat Ryczek, October 12, 1984.) So waiting times can be shortened by talking with the "powers that be."

The use of calendars to structure the work of court personnel is, of course, nothing new. It is routinely done for judges, and as has just been discussed, for commissioners. In fact, in addition to placing cases on the calendar, the personnel in the office just described make sure that all the ingredients are present to constitute a "case." As they do this, personnel fulfill an important screening function, separating cases from non-cases, and in the situation of persons who file their own divorce papers, tell them what officially constitutes a case. This screening function is an important task for lower level street-level bureaucrats (Lipsky, 1980: 128-29).

Both Lipsky (1980) and Prottas (1979) point out that an ongoing problem for organizations which employ street-level bureaucrats is how to exercise control over their work. Calendars and production quotas are devices used to induce reasonable levels of performance. But the unpredictability of street-level work as seen in the complexity of problems presented, lack of normative guidelines for solutions, and the constant dilemma of deciding how much attention can be paid to the individual case in relation to the caseload makes control of street-level work by the organization very difficult. As will be seen later, commissioners, as a whole, have been charged with not handling their calendars efficiently and simply not being productive.

While the scheduling office serves an important function, many persons appearing before the commissioner have no contact with this office, their attorney having made the appointment for them. These clients walk past this office, passing through a short hallway with two windows and chairs lining one side.

One now enters a large, thirty foot by forty foot waiting area. The walls are a pale green and there is one with windows which looks out on courthouse walls. Two oil paintings—one of the first family court commissioners of Milwaukee County, who orginally handled divorce proceedings through the district attorney's office, Jeremiah Kelly and another of Joseph Syman, Family Court Commissioner from 1962-74, are the only pictures. Several wooden tables with wooden chairs along them are often used for brief meetings by attorneys and clients. There are brightly colored chairs along the walls and several rows of chairs in the waiting area itself. Buffed light gray floors and fluorescent lights brighten the area. To persons coming to the commissioner's offices for the first time and observing this area, it is an array of people, most of whom are waiting, discussing both personal and official matters, with receptionists and secretaries moving about trying to facilitate the flow of business. Against one wall at a desk is stationed a deputy sheriff who is available should trouble arise in this area or in one of the commissioners' hearing rooms. The deputy sheriff serves as a reminder to all that overstepping norms of what is considered to be appropriate here will not be tolerated. As one enters the waiting area, immediately to one's right is a receptionist's semi-circular counter with plexi-glass as a divider. When all parties are ready, the commissioner who is hearing the motion is notified by way of intercom, and the parties proceed to the hearing room when informed to do so by the receptionist. When finished with the hearing, the commissioner notifies the receptionist that he/she is finished and whether or not the next motion can be taken. Pertinent court records have also been pulled prior to the hearing by personnel in the receptionist's area so that the commissioner can review the case and later enter his findings and give them to the clerical staff for typing into the record.

In contrast to family courtrooms where persons frequently wait in the back of the courtroom prior to their case being called and talk softly, the waiting area for the commissioners is less quiet. Attorneys may confer with each other about the case at hand or discuss their last vacation. Ex-spouses may be careful to sit at a distance from each other, or some will use the waiting time to discuss how their children are doing. Some browse through magazines. Commissioners can be seen entering the waiting area to discuss some matters with attorneys, greet attorney friends, catch up on courthouse gossip, or just look to see what's happening. Toward the end of the day the crowds thin here—an indication that people have been taken care of. As one secretary put it, "This job is not easy—trying to get rid of people—it's not paper. There's no such thing as putting things in an in-out box here." (Personal Interview with Mary Schmidt, September 26, 1984.)

As one views the waiting area, one is reminded that the street-level bureaucrat controls the pace of his/her work as both Lipsky (1980) and Prottas (1979) have pointed out. The twin tasks of responding to the needs of the individual in light of the demands of the caseload as discussed by Emerson (1983: 426-427) are worked on daily by commissioners who determine to an extent how much time people spend in their waiting area.

Walking past the waiting area, one enters a corridor off of which are located the chief commissioner's hearing room and adjoining office and several other hearing rooms. Only the chief commissioner has a separate office lined with law books and a large conference table in the middle; other commissioners do not have a separate office. Down another hallway from these offices are located two other hearing rooms; also located in this area are the desks of clerical personnel and supervisors who do typing and clerical work for the commissioners. Due to expansion of the staff of commissioners, two other hearing rooms are located on the other side of the waiting area. Paternity hearings are held on the third floor of the courthouse in what was once a courtroom.

While hearing rooms differ in size with the average being twenty-five by twenty feet, in all rooms commissioners sit on an elevated platform behind a desk where a railing above the desk hides papers from view. There are two tables with chairs in front of the commissioner where opposing attorneys and their clients sit. Usually one row of chairs lines the rear of the room which is brightly lit with fluorescent lights. Some hearing rooms have comfortable vinyl-covered chairs while others have wooden ones. The commissioner sits in a high-back chair and wears a business suit or a dress—robes are worn only by the judges. All hearings are open to the public and on occasion a friend or two of the parties involved in the motion will attend.

This is the work environment of the commissioners. It is less formal than a courtroom and more hectic and fast-paced. It is a bewildering array of people coming, going, and waiting for an encounter with a commissioner. It is from this vantage point that commissioners go about explaining what their work consists of.

Internal-Personal Accounts

Maynard (1983: 237) identified the judicial encounter as a concept "where involved parties officially dispose of individual cases." This idea was used in Chapter Four to examine judges' accounts regarding persons involved in this encounter—litigants and attorneys. While commissioners clearly have less power than judges at the court, they are also involved in the processing of cases where litigants and attorneys are the participants. The case processing which commissioners do serves to assist the judges in their work, as the following comment illustrates: "Judges are glad to have the Office of Family Court Commissioners. Our dealing with immediate kinds of problems gives them time to deal with more sophisticated legal stuff." (Personal Interview with Commissioner Randall Davis, October 12, 1984.) So the division of labor which is apparent at the court is that the judges handle the most complex legal matters, as defined by the particular jurisdiction where the court is located. For example, a child custody trial takes place before the judge; commissioners handle less complex, but still pressing problems, as matters of support and visitation. Social workers, as discussed in Chapter Five, are the court's empiricists; they gather information about clients and families. This information is made use of by judges and commissioners to expand their knowledge of the case, and then they use portions of the material presented to reach a decision.

First Hearings. While commissioners may deal with more mundane legal matters than judges, the importance of first hearings over which commissioners preside is a crucial part of the divorce process. If divorcing couples cannot decide upon the terms under which they will live prior to the actual divorce, they need to appear before the commissioner at a hearing where decisions regarding support, custody, and visitation will be made. Several internal-personal accounts refer to litigants at first hearings and how commissioners' organizational work takes place at these hearings.

> We're the first trench for people. At initial hearings they hate each other . . . maybe there are problems with alcohol or a third party. They have to have an opportunity to be heard. They need to have a commissioner who is willing to hear them and to be compassionate. I think at times we are self-appointed psychologists. We have commissioners who have nice things said about them—"He heard me out." (Personal Interview with Commissioner Herbert Steiner, September 27, 1984.)

At first hearings commissioners perceive litigants as being emotionally fragile and having a need to present their side of matters. The role of the commissioner is shaped by the emotional state of these persons, and the commissioner responds as a compassionate listener.

Organizationally, more time is alloted for first hearings—thirty minutes as opposed to fifteen minutes for other hearings—so that the proceeding is not only legal in nature, but also a hearing in which clients' emotional needs can be listened to. The commissioners' dual role of legal expert and "self-appointed" psychologist is evident in initial hearings.

Commissioners are also aware of the role which they play in socializing clients to the legal system of the court, as the following illustrates:

> At the first hearing there's prejudgment work. People are angry, hurt, befuddled. It's important how they're dealt with. If it's in an institutional manner, we can have a damaging effect for years to come. We can have a stabilizing effect also. A constant problem here is the volume. In divorce you're dealing with people who are vulnerable—it's Armageddon early. I like sitting down and talking to these people. It's healthy people going through an insane period. (Personal Interview with Don Murray, Court Commissioner, November 1, 1984.)

Here the commissioner recognizes that the emotional turmoil which people are experiencing is not due to problems of mental imbalance—they are basically healthy people going through a traumatic period. In response to these persons who are suffering emotionally, the commissioner responds sympathetically. However, by doing this the commissioner is performing important organizational work—assisting persons to look at the court favorably, perhaps abetting future problems for the court in dealing with these individuals.

Yet initial hearings are not simply occasions during which commissioners respond to the emotional needs of clients, listening to their stories. Commissioners make important decisions which affect the living arrangements of children, as the following illustrates.

> I had a lady come to me in the summer of 1982. I was a lecturer at the state bar convention. She came up and said, "A year and a half ago I was before you and you talked me into joint custody—I told you at the time that you didn't know what you were doing, but it worked out . . ." When I make a decision in my mind about joint custody I ask myself whether the alternative to joint custody would destroy the child's relationship with the non-custodial parent—that's an important consideration. (Personal Interview with Commissioner Herbert Steiner, September 27, 1984.)

While the commissioner processes individual cases, one at a time, decision making regarding the individual takes into consideration not only the individual person but the social context of that individual, as the above comments illustrate. Social workers in the court make available to commissioners and judges custody evaluations and recommendations about which parent should obtain custody, but at a first hearing this information is only one factor that is considered in terms of a custody decision. As the preceding account makes clear, it is the person seen within a social context which serves as a key basis for the commissioner's discretion in making a decision.

Handling an initial hearing effectively is not only helpful to clients but it makes processing of these individuals move more smoothly as the following illustrates.

> When they're at trial they've had time to cool down. Here [at initial hearings] they're still at each other's throats—sometimes you can feel the tension in the air. (Personal Interview with Commissioner Liz Borkin, October 11, 1984.)

Of course not all initial hearings are volatile and laden with emotion; in fact, the three initial hearings which I observed were calm proceedings where all parties readily agreed. The following statements make this clear.

> *Attorney Smith:* "We've figured out the numbers [regarding support] so I think this should be one of your easier cases today."
>
> *Commissioner Davis:* "I want to commend the parties for working together—I think it will be to the kids' benefit for you to work together, as you have."
>
> (Observation in the hearing room of Commissioner Russell Davis, October 12, 1984.)

Other Hearings. While initial hearings are important since it is here that the conditions under which the divorcing couple will live are decided upon, the great majority of hearings deal with the enforcement of post-divorce decrees. Many of these hearings are of short duration—some less than fifteen minutes and others even less than five minutes. Milewski (1971: 479) indicates that in the bureaucraticized court one means of reducing caseload pressures are "encounters of short duration." This service method is in use in the family court. What follows are excerpts from two hearings conducted by Commissioner Phillips. One hearing deals with a matter of non-support and the other is concerned with a visitation issue; each hearing lasted about five minutes. In the following dialogue, references to personal and ideological factors are used to reach a decision which "makes sense."

A man in his mid-thirties with a ruddy complexion wearing rumpled gray slacks and a brown jacket, call him J.L., appears before Commissioner Phillips in his hearing room. He reviews J.L.'s court record which indicates that he appeared before Phillips about a year ago on a similar matter—non-payment of support. Phillips has a sharp memory, and he indicates that he remembers the man's unusual last name from his previous appearance. J.L. nervously explains, almost in tears, that he hasn't worked since January, 1982.

> *J.L.:* I'm on welfare. I have another wife and two children at home. I've been looking all over for a job and I have this list of places where I've applied (as he shows the list to the Commissioner who reviews it). I hate being on welfare—I want to work, I want to support my family, but I can't find a job.
>
> *M.P.:* That's tough, really tough. You can't give up. I know things are bad. You have to look at the bright side. Eventually something has to happen to turn around our economy. Think positive, that's the way you have to look at it. Look at it from a different perspective. I know that's easy for me to say since I have a job, and I'm earning money.
>
> *J.L.:* I try to do my best.
>
> *M.P.:* I'm not criticizing you—I'm not finding fault.
>
> *J.L.:* I stood in line at A.O. Smith and competed with 15,000 other people for a job. [A.O. Smith is a local Milwaukee firm which advertised that it would be hiring several hundred people—15,000 persons applied.]
>
> *M.P.:* That's good. It shows you're trying. We won't do anything to you as long as you try. You have to believe that unemployment is not all your fault. Factory closing and high prices are the fault of society. But I want to see you again in May—I hope by then you have a job. Keep looking and complete this job search form. [The commissioner hands J.L. a standard job search form on which the man is to get signatures and dates indicating those firms where he has applied for work.]
>
> J.L. smiles, thanks the commissioner and leaves the hearing room. (Personal Observation in Hearing Room of Commissioner Michael Phillips, February 14, 1983.)

Here the commissioner's organizational work consists of processing a case by ascertaining the facts, telling J.L. to follow through on a required job search, and providing psychological support. The role of the commissioner is constructed in large part on the basis of his view of this individual as being contrite yet willing to try to improve his lot. The commissioner responds by offering J.L. reassurance that things will be better and with a marked ideological twist does not "blame the victim" for his unemployment, but notes the problem of unemployment is a societal one.

In a sense the commissioner makes a determination of the individual's moral character, finding him blameless for his unemployment. The process by which bureaucrats assess the moral character of clients is detailed by Emerson (1969: 100) in his study of the juvenile court.

In another hearing of brief duration a couple in their mid-twenties appears before Commissioner Phillips. They had appeared before him previously in a visitation dispute four months ago. Mr. N. had accused Mrs. N. of making it too difficult for him to visit their three-year-old son, Neil. Mrs. N. insisted that she needed more notice from him for a visit. Phillips wanted them to work out suitable visiting arrangements and report back to him. The couple reports that the arrangements are working out well and Phillips compliments them on this,

> I feel confident that you won't have a problem again working out visitation. I want to thank you for being so cooperative. (Observation in Hearing Room of Chief Commissioner Michael Phillips, February 14, 1982.)

After the couple left, Phillips told me that he felt good about this case, that the problem had been Mrs. N.'s unwillingness to let her husband visit his son. Phillips stated,

> If she had a battery of lawyers and objected to her husband seeing his son, I would still want him to be able to visit his father. She could get a battery of lawyers, but she wouldn't change my mind about that. If she tried, I'd sign a contempt order and have her in jail, and then she would change her mind. (Personal Interview with Commissioner Michael Phillips, February 14, 1984.)

In the judicial encounter just described, the commissioner explains his organizational work with primary reference to the persons before him. He presented to them the task of working out a visitation arrangement. This was done and no further legal intervention was necessary; the parties worked out matters themselves, and the commissioner gave his blessings. However, note the commissioner's reaction if Mrs. N. would still have objected to the father's visiting his son. Mrs. N. would be viewed then as being in contempt and subject to being jailed. The commissioner's strong belief that the non-custodial parent should have access to the child would lead him to perform an organizational role of strict enforcer of the law should the custodial parent object to visitation. In the commissioner's statement above, he explains his role toward the mother on the basis of his belief in the rights of the non-custodial parent—in this case, if the woman would not have allowed visitation, Phillips would have labeled her as violating the law and subjected her to prosecution. Finally, the commissioner's strong commitment to the belief that a child should have contact with both parents leads him to act unilaterally, not calling upon the court's social worker to investigate why the mother may not permit her son to visit his father. Thus, in spite of social worker's being assigned the organizational role of assessing what is in the best interest of the child, commissioners exercise discretion as to when to call upon another professional's assessments.

In summary, commissioners' internal-personal accounts deal with individuals involved in divorce, custody, support, and visitation matters. Commissioners are attuned to the emotional needs of clients at initial hearings and take time to hear them out, believing that it is beneficial for the clients and will also make their future contact with the court system easier if they are fairly dealt with. In contrast, judges who recognize the emotional needs of clients see themselves as having little time to respond to these needs (see Chapter Four, p. 53). Social workers, on the other hand, complain about the disorganized, unpredictable way in which clients present their personal difficulties (Chapter Five, p. 77). Commissioners do not voice this complaint and believe that clients' presentation of troubles makes sense, given their situation.

External-Personal Accounts

These accounts deal with attorneys, who in addition to clients, participate in the judicial encounter. Attorneys shape the organizational role of commissioners as the following indicates:

> If you don't grasp things quickly, attorneys can take you for a ride. But they're really not devious. . . I don't want to be taken for a ride, but I don't want to offend the attorneys by cutting them off. (Personal Interview with Commissioner Russell Davis, October 12, 1984.)

As this makes clear, attorneys can be a source of organizational difficulty for commissioners in their work, and so the response of the commissioner is to let attorneys have their say, but be attentive enough so that deviousness doesn't prevail.

Informal controls are used by commissioners to make sure that attorneys do not hamper proceedings, as seen in the following.

> Sometimes attorneys are real competitive, but most of the time when they pick up the cue from the commissioner, they will cooperate. (Personal Interview with Commissioner Russell Davis, October 12, 1984.)

Thus, attorneys' actions in the hearing room are seen as a possible threat to the smooth processing of cases. Commissioners' control of attorneys seems to be less formal than the control exercised by judges, who routinely develop administrative guidelines for attorneys' conduct in courtrooms. (See Chapter Four, p. 55.)

Internal-Organization Accounts

Accounts by Administrators. Prottas (1979: 11) has remarked that a perennial problem for street-level bureaucrats is getting bureaucrats to comply with organizational rules. In order to do this, the bureaucracy must define acceptable levels of a job performance, relate the actual to the ideal performance, and finally, distribute rewards and sanctions according to its evaluations. Public service bureaucracies are notoriously weak at all three tasks.

In discussing such organizational matters with Chief Family Court Judge Susan Samson, she did not indicate any concerns that fellow judges were not working up to job expectations. Three of the four judges met regularly (Chapter Four, p. 55) to discuss administrative problems in their courtrooms, and this practice seems to indicate that this served as an opportunity for the chief judge to be aware of problem areas and to deal with them with her fellow judges. Bob Frances indicated in Chapter Five (p. 68) that he would assume that his staff was doing their work and would not provide supervision or case consultation unless asked. The assumption was that the staff was able to function within the organization as autonomous professionals.

In contrast to these views which do not see compliance as a problem, internal-organization accounts of Commissioner Phillips about commissioners indicate problems of compliance to bureaucratic norms. Commissioner Phillips remarks,

> The biggest problem is dealing with my peers. I have a feeling that they think they're in a special class—"I'm a professional." It's difficult to handle conflict. I tell them—"the rules apply to you as a lawyer, as to a cleaning lady." I've heard some say, "I'm the commissioner." (Personal Interview with Commissioner Michael Phillips, September 27, 1984.)

Explanations about the role which supervisors serve in a public service bureaucracy can take several forms, ranging from the supervisor as enforcer of bureaucratic norms to the supervisor who lets employees function as they wish, assuming that work is being done, provided he/she hears no complaints to the contrary. In the above quotation, the commissioner sees himself as needing to enforce bureaucratic norms and in this way doing organizational work. The rationality which is apparent is adherence to bureaucratic norms on the part of all employees. This is resisted by professionals who see themselves as being more autonomous, as being less bound than non-professionals to "the rules." While street-level bureaucrats cherish autonomy in order to perform their work, the issue of autonomy becomes even more acute for such professionals as lawyers (commissioners) in public service bureaucracies when they have been socialized in professional training to view themselves as autonomous professionals (Hall, 1968; Daniels, 1973: 39).

Another administrator at the court goes on to talk about what for him are organizational difficulties.

> My biggest problem is getting eight hours of work [per day] from them—we have a couple that don't screw off. But that's the nature of working for the county . . . you can't fire or discipline anybody. You have people here who screw off. The quality of work is the same—the quantity is affected. Two people here could do the work . . . but they have their own union—nothing will be accomplished in county government because of the unions. And all these management courses are just a waste of time. County government is in bad shape as far as getting work out—we could get our work done if we had the same supervision system as private industry. Here everybody is afraid that he's going to do more work than someone else.

In this account and the previous one, explanations for getting staff to conform to bureaucratic work norms are offered. Implied is the fact that these problems are due to personal characteristics of family court employees. But in the second description of his oganizational problems with court employees, the analysis of the problem is widened, in essence, using an external-organization account to shift the focus away from one specific area. The focus of the difficulty is seen in a powerful union which in his view rewards minimum levels of productivity. Finally, an external-ideological account is introduced. It is the belief system, espoused in county government, that low levels of production are the norm. While the administrator sees the productivity, or lack thereof as a problem, he maintains that the quality of work is not affected, and in this way he really defends the competence of his staff. Although any department administrator's role is to make sure that his staff is productive, the above accounts cite organizational and ideological factors to justify the current state of matters in one department and in the process, the administrator is seen as acting in a manner which he can justify.

Accounts by Other Commissioners. Issues of productivity have been raised from time to time in all departments of the court. As will be recalled, in Chapter Four, the volume of cases handled by Judges Foley and Hansen became a major concern on the part of those who wanted greater productivity. Commissioners are well aware of the pressure upon them to process more cases. As one commissioner commented, "I suppose *The Milwaukee Journal* will be doing an investigation here again, and the upshot will be that they'll want us to see more people." (Personal Interview with Commissioner Don Murray, November 1, 1984.)

Commissioners, of course, in the interviews did not feel that production was the real issue in their work and none admitted to being nonproductive! Rather, commissioners explain their work productivity by making references to each case as being unique, and their seldom knowing what direction a particular case will take. The emphasis in the family court is on conflict resolution rather than on rule enforcement, the goal of highly bureaucraticized criminal courts (Mileski, 1971: 481), for example.

In discussing the court as an organization and its impact on their work, commissioners view conditions of work as being important. Several examples follow.

> Ultimately it is important who sits here; commissioners need to be rotated—this is a demanding area—one can become jaded and jaundiced. This is the place for burnout. Judges and commissioners need special training in their areas . . . they need to speak before organizations more often and coordinate other support services as social work and psychological services. (Personal Interview with Commissioner Don Murray, November 1, 1984.)

Here burnout, seen as difficulty in actively fulfilling an organizational role, is attributed to conditions of work. While the conditions of work leading to burnout are not spelled out, some suggestions are made for improving the street-level bureaucrat's ability to cope more effectively with organizational demands. The suggestions made are rotation of assignments, special training for family judges and commissioners, and greater contact with, and subsequent awareness of, community needs.

While these suggestions may involve some organizational rearrangements, another account mentions how the time sequence of case processing places organizational demands on commissioners. As mentioned earlier, (p. 105) the commissioner exercises some control over the amount of time spent on a case, but a case may unfold in such a manner that either a greater or lesser amount of time is spent on a case. It is difficult to use short periods of time, as one commissioner comments, "If you get 15-20 minutes, it's hard to psychologically use that time." (Personal Interview with Commissioner Randall Davis, September 21, 1984.)

Both Lipsky (1980: 27) and Emerson (1983: 436) comment that in street-level bureaucracies, time and energy are chronically inadequate relative to tasks. However, work in bureaucracies is not incessant; if a case is adjourned, there may be fifteen to twenty minutes free. While it may be hard to psychologically use that time, the street-level bureaucrat may use it as she/he sees fit—catch up on the backlog of work, plan for the next case, or read the newspaper. Gaps in the work day and how to use them are under the control of the street-level bureaucrat.

A final example of how organizational practices shape the work role of the commissioner is found in the manner in which commissioners do their work. Both Lipsky (1980) and Prottas (1979) have placed considerable emphasis upon the fact that street-level bureaucrats work in isolation, with the police officer being the typical example. While much of what professionals do at the court is done alone, fellow peers are an important reference group for professionals, as Wilensky (1964) has indicated, Commissioners assist one another in managing their work. For example, I was interviewing a commissioner when she received a phone call from a fellow commissioner who asked for some advice regarding how to handle a particular support issue. The commissioner left his hearing room to meet with his colleague and then discussed with her how the matter should be handled. One commissioner told the other how she handled a similar case and how it worked out well. The commissioner returned to his hearing room better equipped to deal with the matter at hand. Peer consultation is common work practice among commissioners and serves to reduce isolation and makes the work role of the commissioners more manageable. In addition, their consulting with one another reduces the risk of making a poor decision which may create greater difficulties.

External-Organizational Accounts

Discussed in Chapter Four was the fact that judges' accounts of organizations external to the court are problematic to them in their work. For example, the legislature is seen as undermining judicial discretion by the use of the word "shall" in state statutes. Social workers' accounts about the finance committee of the county board reveal how the department was reduced in size by 50 percent in large part because of dissatisfaction as to how the director at that time was handling matters (See Chapter Five, p. 67).

Similar to judges and social workers, commissioners' accounts of organizations external to the court view the organizations as making commissioners' work roles problematic. For example,

> There is tremendous pressure on us to set and enforce child support. With child support, the legislature has identified a problem and imposed a solution in terms of what child support levels should be. The impetus, of course, is to take away our discretion. The legislature's question always is, "Is what we're doing playing well before the people?" (Personal Interview with Commissioner Don Murray, November 1, 1984.)

The legislature is seen as undermining the commissioner's discretion and autonomy by making hard and fast rules as to what support levels should be. The dilemma for the commissioner, in performing his organizational role, of course, is whether or not to strictly follow the percentage of income guidelines for support or to make use of discretion and to interpret these guidelines in the light of each case.

One commissioner indicated that if she would follow the state guidelines in a support matter, the man in the case would have been forced to live on only $15.00 per week. In commenting on this case, the commissioner stated, "Discretion is simply necessary in arriving at support levels." (Personal Interview with Commissioner Ellen Branden, October 4, 1984.)

Hasenfeld (1972: 63) comments that organizations which exercise control over people-processing organizations by means of legal statutes create dilemmas for bureaucrats in terms of how to process clients. This is indeed the case for both commissioners and judges who need to weigh the demands of the law on the one hand and the judicious application of discretion on the other.

Internal-Ideological Accounts

Commissioners' accounts of what the court should be shape their organizational work as the following illustrates.

> One of our chief roles is to educate the people as to what should be happening. It's trying to help people realize that they can negotiate matters themselves. There's an incredible number of people who will respond to that and make matters work out. . . I believe that if this is one of the few contacts that people will have with the court system, that people should leave with a sense of fairness. (Personal Interview with Commissioner Russell Davis, October 12, 1984.)

This account is similar to judges' accounts in Chapter Four (p. 61) which also view education regarding individual's rights and obligations under the law as being an important function of the contemporary court. The emphasis is on the role of the legal professional as an enabler, assisting individuals to calculate the impact of the law upon them and thus presumably to act in a manner of enlightened self-interest.

In contrast to judges and commissioners whose accounts in this area are quite straight-forward and similar, social workers' accounts are quite complex. This complexity reflects the idea that the court expects them to fulfill many functions—child welfare advocates, investigators, and therapists—with subsequent confusion on the part of the social workers as to how all of these roles are to be handled, given the existence of many organizational constraints.

External-Ideological Accounts

It was pointed out in Chapter Four that judges' external-ideological accounts deal with the lack of commitment to family values in American society and the concommitant lack of discipline needed to make family life stable. While these accounts centered on the "tradition" of the family, Judge Alexander's accounts in this area see all of society's ills as due to the conflict between forces undermining discipline and those forces which emphasize commitment to one's country, duty, and family. (See Chapter Four, p. 63.) He sees his role as upholding these traditional values.

Commissioners' accounts do not deal with the matters just mentioned; rather their external-ideological accounts deal with the impact of "external" bureaucracies on their work role. Bureaucracy here does not mean a specific organization, but rather a particular world view which espouses a precise, routinized way of handling certain cases. This manner of dealing with cases is most clearly seen in support issues. Commissioner Phillips remarked, "The setting of support is a big issue in the commissioner's office." (Personal Interview with Commissioner Michael Phillips, September 27, 1984.) While the percentage of income guidelines set by the state of Wisconsin is to be used in establishing support, commissioners emphasize that these guidelines cannot be routinely applied to each case. Commissioners fear that bureaucratic guidelines will in the future be used to deal with custody and visitation issues. Their concern is expressed succinctly, "I think the bureaucrats are gradually taking discretion out of the hands of the commissioners and judges." (Personal Interview with Commissioner Herbert Steiner, September 27, 1984.) While the spector of bureaucratic encroachment may loom large for the commissioners, they have been able to operate autonomously in terms of controlling the conditions of their work and exercising discretion. Appeals of commissioners' decisions are rare and only about 1 percent of all decisions are appealed.

Controlling Commissioners' Work

The accounts given by commissioners to make sense of and bring rationality to what they do indicate that they try hard to maintain control over their work environment. It was observed in Chapters Four and Five that this is also the case with judges and social workers who need to maintain their autonomy as professionals. However, other individuals and groups which have observed the practices of professionals at the court, have been critical about the way they go about doing their work. For example, it was noted in Chapter Two (pp. 22-23) that in the 1960's, Judges Hansen and Foley were criticized for dominating the work of the family court with their particular philosophy of what the court should be. They were also criticized for not handling enough cases when they were on the bench. For some time after Hansen and Foley left the family court, judges were appointed for a one year term so as to lessen the possibility of anyone strongly influencing the work of the court with a particular philosophy. It was also observed in Chapter Five (p. 67) that the work of social workers and in particular the work of the director of the Family Reconciliation Department at that time was criticized by judges and lawyers in the community. This criticism eventually found its way to the finance committee of the Milwaukee County Board of Supervisors which reacted by removing the director of the department and reducing the staff by about 50 percent.

As attempts have been made to control the ways in which judges and social workers do their work at the court, so efforts have also been made to bring the work of the commissioners under greater bureaucratic control.

In early April, 1985, both *The Milwaukee Journal* and the *Milwaukee Sentinel* reported the results of a Milwaukee County audit which was done on the office of the Family Court Commissioner. On April 3, 1985, the front page headline in the *Milwaukee Sentinel* read "Audit Rips Free Time in Family Court Day." The audit, which investigated the workings of the office of the Family Court Commissioner, was apparently prompted by the slowness with which child support funds were being collected by the commissioner's office. Timothey J. Riordan, the Milwaukee County Director of Child Support Enforcement, is responsible for seeing to it that the collection of child support monies conforms to state and federal guidelines. He has often been at odds with the commissioners over the scheduling of child support cases (*Milwaukee Sentinel,* August 15, 1985) and was a key figure in bringing about the auditing of the Commissioner's office. Auditors reviewed commissioners' calendars for the months of January and February, 1985, sat in on hearings, interviewed Chief Circuit Court Judge Victor Manian, Commissioner Phillips and his assistants, and surveyed practices of commissioners' offices in ten other counties in Wisconsin.

The audit was most critical of the commissioners' poorly planned work schedule. (An overview of the scheduling of the commissioners' time was presented earlier in this chapter—see pp. 100-101.) The audit indicated that each day, for each commissioner, two hours that are scheduled for hearings are cancelled by lawyers or clients. In addition, an hour and a half during the early mornings and late afternoons is not scheduled. Commissioners contend that the times in which they are not in hearings are spent on correspondence, telephone calls, and legal research. The audit suggested that commissioners worked only four and a half hour days. When informed of this Commissioner Phillips said, "Why, that's absolutely unheard of. If that were the case, we'd have everyone in the county applying for these jobs. It would be paradise over here." (*The Milwaukee Journal,* April 4, 1985.)

Yet Phillips agreed that certain changes would help to improve the functioning of the commissioner's office. Among these was the use of a "master calendar" in which cases would be scheduled for time slots and handled by any commissioner available—as opposed to the current arrangement whereby calendar time slots are booked by individual commissioners. In addition it was recommended that calendars should be overbooked in anticipation of cancelled hearings. In this way commissioners could make up for time that is lost when hearings are cancelled. Phillips ordered that as of April 15, 1985, the commissioner's office would overbook by 30 percent. (*The Milwaukee Journal,* April 4, 1985.)

In addition, the audit of the commissioner's office recommended that court history records should be computerized for future hearings. Also it was recommended that the deputy and assistant family court commissioners should be appointed by the chief commissioner and not by the Chief Circuit Court Judge, so as to enhance the authority of the chief commissioner.

In contrast to the administrative realignments suggested for the commissioner's office, both Chief Circuit Court Judge Victor Manian and Commissioner Phillips, who acknowledge problems in the commissioner's office, have taken a different approach toward dealing with the difficulties. Manian did his own investigation of sorts. He observed in the waiting area of the family commissioners' offices which was described on pp. 100-103. He concluded that people were waiting too long for hearings. "If need be," Manian said, "I'll sit up there and direct traffic and walk up and down the corridors." (*Milwaukee Sentinel,* April 2, 1985.) Manian also talked with some of the commissioners about their responsibility to the public and their duty to promptly be available for hearings. Manian said that if commissioners leave their hearing rooms when they should be conducting hearings, they would be subject to discipline. He said he was considering requiring commissioners to sign in and out when they enter and leave their hearing rooms (*Milwaukee Sentinel,* April 2, 1985).

The chief commissioner complained in response to the findings of the audit, that he is relatively powerless to discipline commissioners and gain control of them. He pointed out the disciplinary action is controlled by civil service regulations, and that he has little authority to deal with his staff (*Milwaukee Sentinel,* April 2, 1985). This analysis is similar to the comments made to me by the chief commissioner.

While administrative changes may improve the productivity of the commissioners, apparently little control can be exercised directly over the work functioning of these professionals. This is made clear in the chief commissioner's perception of his role as noted above. In addition, the chief judge's mode of surveillance of the commissioners continues to construct their own rationality to explain what they do, often quite separate from the demands of the formal organization of which they still are a part. The world of work which the commissioners have constructed exemplifies the power which they, as street-level bureaucrats, have to operate within the court as autonomous professionals.

Summary

The court commissioners are the largest professional group at the family court. They handle a substantial number of motions—22,280 in 1983—and the office of the Commissioner collected $11,582,168 in support monies in 1983 (see Appendix E). A complex structure has evolved to organize the processing of cases involving scheduling of times, types of cases, and retrieval of records. However, in spite of these attempts to increase the level of efficiency in the Office of the Commissioner, a recent audit indicated that the commissioners as a whole are grossly inefficient. The audit suggested certain procedures, such as double booking of appointments and a master calendar to increase the efficiency of the operation.

It is interesting to note that in this recent audit the quality of the work which the commissioners do was never questioned. It was found that the chief judge of the family court has high praise for the commissioners' work (Chapter Four, p. 57). Appeals of commissioners' decisions are only at about the 1 percent level and the chief commissioner expects this and is not concerned (see p. 116). If commissioners are inefficient, it may be related to poor administrative practices which foster inefficiency; for example, due to the use of individual calendars as opposed to a master calendar.

In my observation of and interviews with commissioners, their desire to do a good job and consider each case thoughtfully was very much in evidence. Other than some comments which indicate this, this is of course, a subjective valuation. The attempts to do a good job become more problematic given the conditions of work of the commissioners. The accounts of their work which commissioners give when compared with judges and social workers indicate that it is the commissioners who seem to have the most difficult conditions of work with which to contend. They see divorcing couples at first hearings when the trauma of impending divorce has just struck, and yet it is in this kind of emotional atmosphere where commissioners must set the rules under which the divorcing couple will live. In contrast, by the time the judge sees the couple, the trauma has eased and the couple can more easily handle their feelings. Social workers, as opposed to commissioners, often have the opportunity to select a few cases from their caseload with whom they can practice the art of therapy. Commissioners do not have these opportunities. In fact, if first hearings are often problematic because of emotional volatility on the part of the divorcing couple, enforcing post-divorce decrees is even more difficult for the commissioners.

Dealing with post-divorce decrees is the major single source of difficulty for the commissioners. Hearings involving post-divorce decrees are a seemingly never ending stream of conflicts about custody, support, and visitation — few are dramatic or even interesting and most do not require collaboration from social workers or judges and so these cases are handled autonomously by the commissioner and at times with some helpful consultation from peers. The work is tedious, yet cases do take some twists and there is some unpredictability which provides release from the recital of human woes. In this kind of environment cynicism and pessimism are the enemies, and the commissioners have fought against these threats by asserting their autonomy, whether it is in case decision making or in the matter of just how much work should be done. They have been largely successful in resisting intrusion into their work practices by the formal organization. Reasons for this may be found in lax administrative practices or the commissioners' need to continually assert their autonomy to prevent being overcome by a chaotic and unpredictable environment.

While judges, social workers, and commissioners have developed distinctive rationalities to explain what they do, it is still necessary to explore how these rationalities are related to the organization as a whole. What do the work practices of these street-level bureaucrats indicate about the family court as a whole and its broader purpose and function? It is these matters which will now be considered.

CONCLUSION

THE BASIC PROBLEM which this study addresses is how to explain the ongoing tension between the formal organization's efforts to maintain rationality based on its purpose, on the one hand, with the need of the organization's professionals to exercise substantial discretion in their work of case processing on the other hand. In the process particular, organizationally-based rationalities are developed. This is what I began with as the discrepancy between ideals and actualities (see Preface, p. vii).

This discrepancy between ideals and actualities is articulated along a number of dimensions—historical, institutional, and organizational. This study pays particular attention to how professionals who routinely encounter these discrepancies in their work roles go about constructing accounts or aligning actions to bridge the gap between organizational ideals and organizational realities. Yet this enterprise has also historical and institutional components which not only impinge on the organization as a whole, but also on the professional work within it.

In what follows, the findings of this research, particularly in regard to the basic problem which has just been discussed, is presented. While this is a case study, some cautious generalizations about the nature of professional work in other people-processing organizations are also made. Theoretical issues are discussed in terms of what this study contributes to organizational theory. Finally, I present some modest suggestions for change in the family court.

Explaining Organizational Discrepancies

As discussed in Chapter Three, p. 32, the formal/rational model of organizations stresses the importance of goals in shaping the behavior of organizational participants. This model can be applied toward the understanding of distinctive human service organizations such as the juvenile court and the family court.

The juvenile court, as I noted in Chapter Two, has been written about thoroughly from both historical and organizational perspectives. This is simply not the case in regard to the family court. For example, although various authors (Alexander, 1956, 1958; Dyson and Dyson, 1969; Zukerman, 1969) have discussed aspects of the history of the development of the family court nationally, no full length history of the family court in the United States has been done. In addition, no studies of the family court as an organization and service provision within it, have been conducted.

On a local level, historical material on the family court is even more meager; there are no published histories of local courts available. In the court under study, its history was pieced together on the basis of one journal article (Hansen, 1966), public relations pamphlets produced by the court, newspaper articles, and interviews with judges who served in the family court for most the 1960's.

Although the social work department in the court under investigation was founded in 1935, little is known of its work between that date and 1960 other than the fact that it worked to bring about reconciliation in those cases where it seemed possible. However, beginning in 1960 this court made a concerted effort to affect reconciliation and to pay special attention to the welfare of children in divorce cases. A guardian ad litem was appointed for children whose parents were involved in custody, support, and visitation issues to determine what was in the best interest of the child. If the family court prior to 1960 did not have an overall purpose, for most of the decade of the 1960's the court under study had clearly defined objectives. These were that a good disposition was reconciliation, that the child was best served through an intact marriage, and that the law is best served by achieving these results. The thrust toward reconciliation was not only present in the jurisdiction under study but also in family courts in Toledo, Cincinnati, and Denver. Of course, the day to day work of professionals in the family court during the 1960's was never studied, so nothing is known regarding how the court's goal of reconciliation influenced the court's work, although some speculation can be made. A report of the work of the court in this study talks about the spirit of partnership that united the disciplines of law and social work (see Appendix A). In addition, in 1967 there appeared in *Social Casework* an article regarding marital counseling and child custody studies in the family court. It was authored by the Chief Family Court Judge and a social worker in the Department of Family Conciliation. The article is reflective of legal and therapeutic efforts to assist families during the era of reconciliation in the court. It is noteworthy that since the 1960's no formal statements about the purpose of the court under study have been made.

While reconciliation appears to be praiseworthy in its efforts to provide assistance for the troubled family and prevent divorce, it must be remembered that the moral order during the era of reconciliation was one of guilt and innocence. Prior to no-fault divorce, a divorce could only be granted to an "innocent party" who was harmed by his or her spouse's violation of the marriage contract. The law required that one party be found "guilty" and the other "innocent." However, as Wheeler (1974) points out, even proof of fault did not guarantee that a divorce would be granted; also if both parties were at fault, neither could obtain a divorce. The morality of guilt and innocence was plagued with contradictions. No doubt reconciliation efforts during the 1960's represented the court's efforts to prevent lengthy legal battles to prove guilt and innocence, thus attempting to avert divorce. In the case of the court under study the fervor of reconciliation during the 1960's also represented attempts to preserve the value of marriage as a lifelong commitment. This seems to have represented an assertion of values which emphasized the importance of maintaining the family unit intact if at all possible. (See Chapter 2, p. 18.) Historically the 1960's in American society was a time of social upheaval and a questioning of traditional values. Perhaps the court's emphasis on reconciliation as articulated by the "Irish priest and Norwegian policeman" was an effort to affirm traditional family values.

Although the moral order prior to no-fault divorce was articulated formally in terms of guilt and innocence, the bitterness, perjury, hostility, and hypocrisy that pervaded the entire divorce process led to reform efforts. In 1970 California instituted the first no-fault divorce law in the western world; by 1985 every state except South Dakota had some type of no-fault divorce. Under no-fault the gender-neutral standards of financial need and ability to pay replaced fault-linked alimony, property, and child support awards of the old laws. Reformers believed that the more realistic economic standards of the new laws would bring about equity, equality, and justice to the process of divorce. In fact, Weitzman (1985) in her study of the effects of no-fault divorce in California, particularly on women and children, indicates that the reformers believed that justice for both parties in a divorce would be better served by considering their economic situations instead of their guilt or innocence.

Weitzman (1985: 338) states that changes in standards of living for divorced men and women in her Los Angeles sample showed a 42 percent increase in income for men but a 73 percent decrease for women. Thus the coming of no-fault brought about a switch from justice based on guilt and innocence to justice based on economic factors. As can readily be seen from the figures just cited, in Weitzman's study post-divorce economic status remains relatively gender-based.

But perhaps even more important than the shift from guilt and innocence to economic factors in divorce was the fact that no-fault divorce reflected a shift in the role of the family court from a position of espousing a moral order which protected marriage by making dissolution difficult (through reconciliation efforts) to one of actually facilitating divorce. As Weitzman (1985: 368) indicates, the new divorce laws adopted a laissez-faire approach toward both marriage and divorce. As a result, the family court was no longer able to enforce the traditional marriage contract through its work of reconciliation.

What kind of moral order emerged to guide the work of the family court under investigation after no-fault? In contrast to the goals of the court during the era of reconciliation, no statement of goals of the court during the last fifteen years could be found. However, in terms of the organizational functioning of the court, a statement cited earlier (see Chapter Two, p. 26) by the chief social worker at the court is noteworthy: "It's [the family court] not an organization; it's four judges, eight commissioners, and seven social workers doing their own thing." Of course the major part of this study has been devoted to the description and analysis of how these professionals go about "doing their own thing." It has been found that what they do is greatly shaped by the organizational niche in which they find themselves, by the need to manage large caseloads and move people along. If a moral consensus exists among professionals in the court it is around the issue of what will happen to the children of divorce; how the court will respond to their needs. Yet the evidence suggests that often these professionals view each other with distrust and suspicion when it comes to making child custody decision. (See Chapter Four, pp. 57-58.)

With few clear normative guidelines from the broader society as to what marriage and criteria for divorce should be (see Bohannan, 1985, for an excellent description of this matter), the court's professionals are often at a loss to know what kind of decision to make. This problem is intensified by the fact that in the case of the law, specific statutes exist but these are always subject to interpretation. As I have illustrated in the case of judges and commissioners, organizational factors such as time constraints significantly influence the decision-making process. In the matter of the social work profession, Popple (1985) has indicated its theoretical weakness. In the case of the social workers in the court, I found no evidence that guiding theoretical frameworks were being used to assist them in decision making. As a result their decision making tends to be highly individualized in nature, and based heavily on their experiences, both professional and personal.

While the lack of normative guidelines influence what professionals do, oganizational factors need also to be examined to understand the discrepancy between the formal organization's thrust toward rationality and organizationally-based rationalities.

The court of reconciliation of the 1960's was led by two judges who believed in the stated mission of the court and seemingly were able to unite the court's professionals under the banner of reconciliation and concern for the welfare of children of divorce. Their successors criticized them for not paying enough attention to productivity issues. Historical material from this period reveals increased emphasis on the importance of processing more cases with greater speed. Following the passage of the no-fault divorce law in 1978, there appears to have been an increase in the number of cases handled by the court (see Appendix C), with some increase of staff but no changes in the program of the court or its administration. No revised goals of the court, taking into consideration the fact of no-fault divorce, were formulated. Obviously new laws continued to be passed but the court as a whole developed no overall framework within which to view itself and its overall purpose. Yet in spite of having no formally stated goals and weak leadership, the family court under study continues to exist. Perhaps it is an example of what Perrow (1979: 198) refers to as those organizations which develop an inner logic and direction of their own in spite of those who appear to control them (or who do not control them!).

In the case of the family court this inner logic and direction consists of the construction by professionals of aligning actions or accounts which permit professionals to make sense out of organizational work life, but are of questionable use to clients in their efforts to reconstruct life after divorce. As long as the historical, institutional, and organizational elements regarding marriage and divorce are in disequilibrium, the ongoing tension between the formal organization's quest for overall rationality and the organizationally based rationalities of professionals will continue. However, in this conflict the professionals and not organizational leaders are clearly in charge.

Work in People-Processing Organizations

It seems clear that following the era of reconciliation, the family court under study became a people-processing organization or street-level bureaucracy. These organizations have already been discussed in considerable detail (see Chapter Three, pp. 36-38). Characteristics of these organizations include unclear goals, limited resources, and a staff who interact daily with clients and must use discretion in making decisions. It might also be added that the unclear goals which these organizations exhibit are based in part in relation to their institutional referrents. Bohannan and Huckleberry (1967) indicate that family courts are greatly influenced by the institutions of divorce, family, and the law. The law has constructed the institution of divorce as a means whereby family breakup is dealt with. While the family court can clarify the legal dimensions of family breakup, the court in and of itself is of little help in assisting families in the task of family reconstruction after divorce.

The lack of clearly defined norms as to what post-divorce social arrangements are to be like has led to individual struggles to "adjust," with professionals facilitating the process. Social innovations in the form of back-up institutions, as Bohannan and Huckleberry (1967: 102) refer to them, are necessary to provide clearer guidelines for post-divorce adjustment.

As noted earlier, the era of people-processing in the family court emerged following the period of reconciliation. The demise of a moral order led to unclear goals for the court and uncertainty regarding what type of framework was to be used to be of assistance to clients. It also appears that the court's caseload increased without a subsequent addition of manpower. Lipsky (1980) points out that a dimunition of resources leads to considerable discretion in rationing services which can result in inequality, favoritism, and alienation in service provisions. These factors were not apparent in this study; rather, on the basis of this study, a number of other characteristics of people-processing emerged.

Individual street-level bureaucrats or professionals are highly concerned about the management of their own caseloads. The legal and social work professions at the court spent hardly any time talking with one another to devise new ways of improving services. Judges and commissioners, however, perhaps because of their common professional background and ability to implement procedural changes, met routinely to discuss such matters at the court.

There is a great deal of uncertainty among the professionals at the court as to what the purpose of their work should be. In this respect the formal/rational model of organizations which stresses highly defined work roles is of little use in understanding professionals in their daily decision making. On the other hand, the institutional school which stresses the importance of an organization's history and its linkages to its environment seems more useful but underestimates the power of individual organizational actors to determine the working rationality of the organization—to this the framework of street-level bureaucracy is a useful corrective.

As I have pointed out, since the court lacks any kind of overall rationality, work itself, as one social worker put it, becomes situational (Chapter Five, p. 92) meaning that work is not part of any broader rationality or purpose. Yet in this anomic atmosphere professionals are expected to function autonomously and use discretion in making decisions which are of great importance for individuals.

Probably professional work in the family court under study as reflected in the accounts of professionals, will have much the same character in time to come if the court has the following characteristics: unclear or lack of organizational goals, weak organizational leadership, unclear institutional goals (in terms of what a good marriage or a good divorce consists of), and limited organizational assets in terms of time and money. The presence of these factors leads to alienated work not only in the family court but also in those organizations with the characteristics just mentioned.

Organizational Theory and the Study

In Chapter Three, several theories of organization—the formal/rational model, the social construction view, and the institutional school—were presented as frameworks to guide the empirical investigation of the family court. What has been learned about organizational theory from this study? And specifically, what is the contribution of this study to organizational theory? Essentially the formal/rational model, the social constructionist view, and the institutional school have been used to understand the functioning of the family court. On the basis of this study, theoretical attention needs to be centered on the relevance of the environment for analyzing organizations.

The formal/rational model as discussed in Chapter Three views the organization as a rationally contrived unit of human association. An assumption of this model is that a purpose or goals is essential for organizational functioning. Based on the research in this study, the family court has functioned since the 1960's (the era of reconciliation) without any clearly articulated goals. In this particular court there is even an absence of goals formulated by specific organizational groups to further, for example, their professional domain. So this study makes clear that organizations continue to exist in spite of the lack of any overall rationality. However, as has been repeatedly pointed out, the price of this is high as reflected in alienation in work among professionals and perhaps as a result, decreased effectiveness as human service providers.

Inspite of the fact that the court as an organization seems anomic in character, one way it is produced through history is by the work of professionals. The social construction view sees organizational actors as having considerable flexibility in their work domains to construct and reproduce organizational work patterns. In the process of their work in the family court, professionals construct multiple rationalities to make sense out of their work and give it meaning. The accounts are interpretations of work which is alienated in character since it reflects the anomic state of the organization itself. Perrow (1979: 246-47) indicates that the social construction approach is useful but somehow needs to be linked to the broader concern of the relationship between the organization and its environment. I have attempted to show these linkages by indicating that the family court is reactive to its institutional environment and since this environment lacks clear normative guidelines, this is reflected both on the formal organizational level and in the accounts of professionals.

The institutional school has long emphasized the importance of the organization's environment. Often this took the form of an emphasis on the equilibrium which the organization achieved with its environment. Perrow (1979: 200) emphasizes that in recent organizational theory there is a renewed emphasis on the role of the environment in understanding organizations. Perrow (1979: 246) sees this in terms of the organization creating, selecting, and defining the environment with a lot of fragmentation in the process.

A more radical view is that of Meyer (1978: 363) who has written extensively on the relationship between the organization and the environment. As he states, "and we ignore the obvious fact that post-industrial society creates vast new forms of certainty, which organizations may obtain by the mere process of conformity to environmental specification." In this study of the family court, there is little indication that the institutions of family, divorce and the law are creating any greater normative clarity to make the work of the court any easier and more meaningful. In fact if organizations merely react to environmental dictates, the result may be increased organizational fragmentation.

This study emphasizes the importance of the institutional environment in understanding the formal organization and the work practices of professionals within it. Although organizations can function without a purpose, these organizations tend to be ineffective and work there is alienated. This research suggests that organizations which have a purpose (as the family court in the era of reconciliation) may produce better work and less alienated workers. There is a need for a family court with a purpose, and this suggests the revival of a Weberian model with emphasis on specific organizational goals. Whether a charismatic leader or a professional elite can define goals, it is uncertain, given the complexity of the institutions which impact upon the court.

Some Modest Suggestions for Change in the Family Court

Writing in 1967, Bohannan and Huckleberry looked at the institutions of divorce, family, and the law in American society. They concluded that the law created the institution of divorce for dealing with conflict within the family. The law in and of itself, however, is inadequate in dealing with the task of family reconstruction. Bohannan and Huckleberry (1967: 101) indicated that as long as Americans maintained the practice of neolocality and preferred a husband-wife based social system that "broken homes" in the absence of new back-up institutions would continue to exist.

In 1985, in *All the Happy Families,* Bohannan once again reviewed the status of the American family and divorce. He concluded that the divorce industry—an amalgam of industries and professions which benefit socially and economically from the piecemeal, individualistic fashion in which our society handles divorce—is thriving. On the other hand, both organizationally and institutionally, American society has done relatively little to create what Bohannan calls a well family industry. Such an endeavor recognizes the fact that good families are the ones that make good children and that good parenthood, not merely a happy marriage, is the essence of a good family and of a good society no matter what form such families take (Bohannan, 1985: 235). With these guidelines new social arrangements need to be created to improve the functioning of changing families.

I have indicated that the family court which I have studied has, after the era of reconciliation, done little to develop an overall organizational rationality to deal with the problems of social reconstruction which families experience in the aftermath of divorce. Certainly the psycho-social problems which both adults and children experience after divorce have been documented repeatedly (Gardner, 1976; Cassetty, Roman and Haddad, 1978; Wallerstein and Kelly, 1980; Weitzman, 1985). Yet I have shown that due to the lack of any organizational purpose the efforts of professionals to be of assistance are individual and *ad hoc* in nature. Therefore it is important for the court to devise programs to help persons dealing with the emotional aftermath of divorce. Although examples of such programs are sparse, some family courts have developed specific programs for assisting families.

A chief drawback of this study is that it is limited to one case. Therefore I have reviewed the literature to see what programs other family courts have devised to address the psycho-social dimensions of family break-up. There is very little reported. Young (1980) discussed a series of court-mandated workshops for adolescent children of divorcing parents conducted in the Family Court of Allen County, (Ft. Wayne) Indiana. Young (1978) also reported the results of a "divorce experience workshop" conducted by the family court of Allen County. Each workshop was four hours in length and conducted over a period of nine weeks. Attendance at this pre-divorce workshop was required of filing spouses with at least one minor child. In evaluating the workshop, 91 percent would participate voluntarily again; 71 percent wanted additional workshop experience, and 90 percent reported they would suggest that a friend attend the program. Consideration of such programs by the court under study may be useful to individuals and may also provide professionals with an area for growth and stimulation.

While no-fault divorce has done much to remove the moral framework of guilt and innocence from divorce, it is important to remember that the law is still practiced within an adversarial context. As a result, one party is pitted against the other in the courtroom arena attempting to gain as much as possible. No doubt in some situations this type of conflict resolution is the only option available to resolve matters. However, various authors have suggested that the adversarial approach is simply inappropriate when applied to the resolution of many marital disputes (Pearson, Thoennes, and Vandekooi, 1982: 18). Bohannan (1970) believes that the use of the adversarial model actually increases trauma and escalates conflict rather than achieving a peaceful resolution. Irving and Irving (1974) argue that an adversarial approach accelerates the emotional trauma that already exists and makes efforts at constructive communication even more difficult.

As a result of the deficiencies of the adversarial approach, mediation is being viewed as an acceptable alternative for resolving family disputes. Essentially mediation is a persuasion technique in which an acceptable third party helps contesting parties reach a mutually agreeable settlement of their differences. Pearson, Thoennes, and Vanderkooi (1982: 20) believe that in comparison with the adversarial system, mediation seems to be more expeditious, less expensive, procedurally reasonable, and amenable to truth-finding and the open airing of differences. In the area of child custody disputes, Ninookin and Kornhauser (1979) found that child adjustment may be impaired by the court. Therefore, child custody matters may be more adequately handled through mediation in which consensual solutions are arrived at.

Various authors (Davidson, 1975; Weiss and Collada, 1977) have advised that family courts establish mediation services. Writing in 1982, Pearson, Thoennes, and Vanderkooi indicated that family courts in thirteen states had established mediation services. In addition private mediation services have arisen. It is becoming an area of cooperative effort for both lawyers and mental health professionals; it seems to be an idea whose time has come. This is an area where legal professionals and social workers could develop expertise and make use of this knowledge to be of assistance in selected cases in the court, particularly child custody matters. A pilot project in the court making use of mediation, especially in regard to custody issues, would be a step in the right direction and could bring professionals in the court into closer, working cooperation.

It does not seem feasible for the family court of the 1980's to unite under a rubric similar to that of the reconciliation concept of the 1960's. However, Rowbottom and Billes (1977) suggest that the internal work environment of an organization can be designed to deal with the different types of work which is done. The court in this study has done an excellent job of collecting support monies, for example. Now it needs to turn its attention to structuring its work environment to assist clients to deal with the emotional aftermath of divorce. Modest, achievable organizational goals need to be once again articulated by the court's professionals.

BIBLIOGRAPHY

Aldrich, Howard E., and Jeffrey Pfeffer. "Environments of Organizations" in *Annual Review of Sociology,* Vol. 2. Palo Alto, California: Annual Review, 1978.

Alexander, Paul W. "Legal Science and the Social Sciences: The Family Court." *Missouri Law Review,* Vol. 21, No. 2, April, 1956: 105-18.

________. "The Family Court—An Obstacle Race." *University of Pittsburgh Law Review.* Vol. 19, 1958: 602-18.

Barnard, Chester I. "Organizations as Systems of Cooperation" in *The Functions of the Executive:* 4-21. Cambridge MA: Harvard University Press, 1938.

Becker, Howard S. and Blanche Geer. "Participant Observation: A Comparison," in George J. McCall and J.L. Simmons, *Issues in Participant Observation,* 322-331. Reading, MA: Addison-Wesley, 1969.

Belkamp, Ivan. *Human Problems of a State Mental Hospital.* New York: McGraw-Hill, 1956.

Berger, Peter L. and Thomas Luckmann. *The Social Construction of Reality.* New York: Doubleday, 1966.

Bohannan, Paul and Karan Huckleberry. "Institutions of Divorce, Family, and the Law," *Law and Society Review* 1, June, 1967: 81-102.

________. *Divorce and After.* Garden City, NJ: Doubleday, 1970.

________. *All the Happy Families: Exploring the Varieties of Family life.* New York: McGraw-Hill, 1985.

Buckholdt, David R. and Jaber F. Gubrium. *Caretakers.* New York: Sage, 1979.

Cassetty, Judith H. *Child Support and Public Policy.* Lexington, MA: Lexington Books, 1978.

Cavan, Ruth Shonle. *Juvenile Delinquency.* 2nd ed. Philadelphia: Lippincott, 1969.

Chudacoff, Howard P. *The Evolution of American Urban Society,* 2nd Edition. Englewood Cliffs, NJ: Prentice-Hall, 1981.

Cicourel, Aaron V. *Method and Measurement in Sociology.* New York: Free Press, 1964.

________, et al. *Language Use and School Performance.* New York: Academic Press, 1974.

________. *The Social Organization of Juvenile Justice.* London: Heinemann, 1976.

Cressey, Donald B. "Doing Justice," *The Center Magazine* 10, January/February, 1977: 22.

Dalton, Melvin. *Men Who Manage.* New York: Wiley, 1959.

Daniels, Arlene Koplan. "How Free Should Professional Be?" Eliot Freidson, ed. *The Professionals and Their Prospects,* 39-57. Beverly Hills: Sage, 1971.

Davidson R. *Marriage and Family Law in Toronto.* Vancouver and Toronto: International Self-Council Press, Ltd., 1975.

Day, L.B. "The Development of the Family Court,": 96-103. From *Selected Essays on Family Law.* Brooklyn: Foundation Press, 1950.

Dean, J.P., R.I. Eichorn and L.R. Dean. "Observation and Interviewing" in J. Doby, *An Introduction to Social Research,* 2nd Ed.: 274-304. Des Moines, IA: Meredith, 1967.

Dee, Jacqueline Hanson, ed. "Family Law." Special edition, *Marquette Law Review,* Spring and Summer, 1983, Vol. 66, nos. 3 and 4.

Denzin, Norman K. *The Research Act.* New York: McGraw-Hill, 1978.

Dinitz, Simon and John P. Conrad. "The Dangerous Two Percent" in *Critical Issues in Juvenile Delinquency.* David Shichor and Delos H. Kelly, editors. Lexington, MA: Lexington Books, 1980.

Dyson, Elizabeth D. and Richard B. Dyson. "Family Courts in the United States." *Journal of Family Law,* May, 1969, Vol. 9: 1-100.

Eisenstein, James and Herbert Jacob. *Felony Justice: An Organizational Analysis of Criminal Courts.* Boston: Little, Brown, 1977.

Emerson, Robert M. and Sheldon L. Messinger. "The Micro-Politics of Trouble." *Social Problems* 25, December, 1977: 121-35.

________. "Holistic Effects in Social Control Decision Making." *Law and Society Review* 17, 3, 1983: 435-55.

________, ed. *Contemporary Field Research.* Boston: Little, Brown, 1977.

Etzioni, Amitai. *A Comparative Analysis of Complex Organizations.* Glencoe, IL: Free Press, 1961.

Fabricant, Michael. *Juveniles in Family Courts.* Lexington, MA: Lexington Books, 1983.

Feeley, Malcolm M. "Two Models of the Criminal Justice System: An Organizational Perspective." *Law and Society Review,* 7, 1973: 407-25.

Foster, H. "Conciliation and Counseling." *New York University Law Review,* Vol. 41, 1966: 355-56.

Gardner, Richard A. *Psychotherapy with Children of Divorce.* New York: J. Aronso, 1976.

Goffman, Erving. *Asylums: Essays on the Social Situation of Mental Patients and Other Inmates.* New York: Doubleday, 1961.

________. *Interaction Ritual.* Garden City, New York: Doubleday, 1967.

Goldstein, A.S. "The State and the Accused: Balance of Advantage in Criminal Procedure." *Yale Law Journal* 69, 1960: 1149-99.

Gordon, William C. "The Family Court: When Properly Defined, It Is Both Desirable and Attainable." *Journal of Family Law,* Vol. 14, 1975: 1-29.

Gouldner, Alvin. *Patterns of Industrial Bureaucracy.* New York: Free Press, 1954.

Gubrium, Jaber F. *Living and Dying at Murray Manor.* New York: St. Martin's Press, 1975.

________. "Institutionalization and the Family." Special edition of *Journal of Family Issues,* December, 1983, Vol. 4, no. 4.

Gulliver, P.H. "Introduction to Case Studies of Law in Non-Western Societies," Neder, Lawn, ed. *Law in Culture and Society.* Chicago: Aldine, 1969: 11-22.

Gusfield, Joseph R. "Social Structure and Moral Reform: A Study of the Women's Christian Temperance Union," *American Journal of Sociology* 61, 1955: 221-32.

Hage, Jerald. *Theories of Organization: Form, Process, and Transformation.* New York: Wiley, 1980.

Hall, Peter M. and John P. Hewitt. "The Quasi-Theory of Communication and the Management of Dissent." *Social Problems* 18, Summer: 17-27.

Hall, Richard H. "Professionalization and Bureaucratization." *American Sociological Review* 33, February, 1968: 92-104.

_______. *Organizations: Structure and Process.* Englewood Cliffs, NJ: Prentice Hall, 1982.

_______. "Theoretical Trends in the Sociology of Professions." *The Sociological Quarterly* 24, Winter, 1983: 5-23.

Hamparian, Donna, Richard L. Schuster, Simon Dinitz, and John P. Conrad. *The Dangerous Few.* Lexington, MA: Lexington Books, 1978.

Hansen, Robert. "Three Dimensions of Divorce." *Marquette Law Review,* Vol. 50, August, 1966, no 1: 1-14.

_______. "Children of Divorce—What Rights Have They?" *Reader's Digest,* March, 1967: 181-86.

_______ and Sidney Goldberg. "Casework in a Family Court." *Social Casework,* Vol. 48, no. 7, July, 1967: 416-421.

Hasenfeld, Yeheskel. "People-Processing Organizations: An Exchange Approach." *American Sociological Review* 37, June, 1972: 256-63.

Heumann, Milton. "A Note on Plea Bargaining and Case Pressure." *Law and Society Review* 9, 1972: 515-28.

Hewitt, John P. and Randall Stokes. "Disclaimers." *American Sociological Review,* 40, February, 1975: 1-11.

Hughes, Everett C. *The Sociological Eye: Selected Papers.* Chicago and New York: Aldine-Atherton, 1971.

Irving, H.H. and B.G. Irving. "Conciliation Counseling in Divorce Litigation." *Reports of Family Law,* 16, 1978: 257-66.

Jacob, Herbert. *Urban Justice: Law and Order in American Cities.* Englewood Cliffs, NJ: Prentice Hall, 1973.

Karger, Howard. "Burnout as Alienation." *Social Service Review,* June, 1981: 270-83.

Kerr, S., M.A. Von Glinow and J. Schriesheim. "Issues in the Study of Professionals in Organizations: The Case of Scientists and Engineers." *Organizational Behavior and Human Performance* 18, 1977: 329-45.

Lefstein, N.V. Stapleton, and L., Teitelbaum. "In Search of Juvenile Justice." *Law and Society Review* 5, 1969: 491-563.

Levine, Murray. *From State Hospital to Psychiatric Center: The Implementation of Organizational Change.* Lexington, MA: Lexington Books, 1980.

Lipsky, Michael. *Street-Level Bureaucracy: Dilemmas of the Individual in Public Services.* New York: Sage, 1980.

Littrell, W. Boyd. *Bureaucratic Justice: Police, Prosecutors, and Plea Bargaining.* Beverly Hills: Sage, 1979.

Lofland, John. *Analyzing Social Settings.* Belmont, CA: Wadsworth, 1971.

Malinowski, Bronislaw, in C.K. Ogden and I.A. Richards, *The Meaning of Meaning.* New York: Harcourt, Brace, 1930: 300-305.

March, James G. *Handbook of Organizations.* Chicago: Rand-McNalley, 1965.

March, James G. and Herbert A. Simon. *Organizations.* New York: Wiley, 1958.

Maynard, Douglas W. "Social Order and Plea Bargaining in the Courtroom." *The Sociological Quarterly* 24, 1983: 233-51.

McCall, George J. and J.L. Simmons. *Issues in Participant Observation.* Reading, MA: Addison-Wesley, 1969.

McKinney, John C. *Constructive Typology and Social Theory.* New York: Appleton-Century-Crofts, 1966.

Medalie, R.J. "Custodial Police Interrogation in Our Nation's Capital: The Attempt to Implement Miranda." *Michigan Law Review* 66, 1968: 1347-1422.

Merton, Robert K. and Patricia L. Dendall. "The Focused Interview," *American Journal of Sociology* 51, May, 1946: 542-57.

Merton, Robert K. "Bureaucratic Structure and Personality," from *Social Theory and Social Structure,* 249-60. Glencoe, IL: Free Press, 1968.

Messinger, Sheldon L. "Organizational Transformation: A Case Study of a Declining Social Movement," *American Sociological Review* 29, 1955: 3-10.

Meyer, John W. and W. Richard Scott. *Organizational Environments: Ritual and Rationality.* Beverly Hills: Sage, 1983.

Meyer, Marshall and Associates. *Environment and Organizations: Theoretical and Empirical Perspectives.* San Francisco: Jossey-Bass, 1978.

Michel, Robert. *Political Parties.* New York: Free Press, 1966.

Mills, C. Wright. "Situated Action and the Vocabulary of Motives." *American Sociological Review* 6, December, 1940: 904-13.

Mileski, Maureen. "Courtroom Encounters: An Observation Study of a Lower Criminal Court." *Law and Society Review,* Vol. 5, 1971: 473-479.

Mnookin, Paul and A. Kornhauser. "Bargaining in the Shadow of the Law: The Case of Divorce." *Yale Law Journal,* 1979: 950.

Morrissey, Joseph F., Howard H. Goldman and L.V. Klerman, eds. *The Enduring Asylum: Cycles of Institutional Reform at Worcester State Hospital.* New York: Grune & Stratton, 1980.

Parsons, Talcott. *Structure and Process in Modern Societies.* Glencoe, IL: Free Press, 1960.

Pearson, Jessica, Nancy Thoennes and Lois Vanderkooi. "The Decision to Mediate." *Journal of Divorce,* Vol. 6. nos. 1 and 2, 1982: 17-36.

Perrow, Charles. *Complex Organizations: A Critical Essay,* 2nd ed. New York: Random House, 1979.

Platt, Anthony. *The Child Savers: The Invention of Delinquency,* Second edition. Chicago Press, 1977.

Popple, Philip R. "The Social Work Profession: A Reconceptualization." *Social Service Review,* Vol. 59, No. 4, December, 1985: 560-577.

Prottas, Jeffrey Manditch. "The Power of the Street-Level Bureaucrat in Public Service Bureaucracies." Harvard University: Department of City and Regional Planning, 1977: 1-29.

________. *People-Processing: The Street-Level Bureaucrat in Public Service Bureaucracies.* Lexington, MA: Lexington Books, 1979.

Rainwater, Lee and David J. Pittman. "Ethical Problems in Studying a Politically Sensitive and Deviant Community," in *Social Problems,* 1967, 14: 357-66.

Ritzer, George. *Sociology: A Multiple Paradigm Science.* Boston: Allyn and Bacon, 1975.

Roman, Mel and William Haddad. *The Disposable Parent: The Case for Joint Custody.* New York: Holt, Rinehart, and Winston, 1978.

Rowbottom, Ralph and David Billes. "The stratification of Work and Organizational Design," *Human Relations* 30, No. 1, 1977: 53-76.

Ryerson, Ellen. *The Best-Laid Plans.* New York: Hill and Wang, 1978.

Schutz, Alfred. *On Phenomenology and Social Relations.* Chicago: University of Chicago Press, 1970.

Scott, Marvin B. and Stanford Lyman. "Accounts." *American Sociological Review* 33, no. 1, February, 1968: 46-62.

Scott, Robert A. "The Selection of Clients by Social Welfare Agencies: The Case of the Blind," *Social Problems* 14, No. 3, Winter, 1967: 148-57.

Scott, W. Richard. "Field Methods in the Study of Organizations," in James G. March, *Handbook of Organizations.* Chicago: Rand-McNalley, 1965: 261-304.

________. "The Organization of Environments: Network, Cultural, and Historical Elements." Meyer, John W. and W. Richard Scott, *Organizational Environments: Ritual and Rationality.* Beverly Hills: Sage, 1983: 155-75.

Seeley, Johen R. *Community Chest.* Toronto: University of Toronto Press, 1957.

Selznick, Philip. *TVA and the Grass Roots.* Berkeley and Los Angeles: University of California Press, 1949.

Shafritz, Jan M. and Philip H. Whitbeck, eds. *Classics of Organization Theory.* Oak Park, IL: Moore, 1978.

Sjoberg, Gideon and Roger Nett. *A Methodology for Social Research.* New York: Harper and Row, 1968.

Skolnick, Jerome. *Justice Without Trial.* New York: Wiley, 1966.

Street, David, Robert Vinter and Charles Perrow. *Organizations for Treatment.* New York: Free press, 1966.

Sudnow, David. "Normal Crimes: Sociological Features of the Penal Code in a Public Defender Office." *Social Problems* 12, 1965: 255-76.

Tappan, Paul. *Delinquent Girls in Court: A Study of the Wayward Minor Court of New York.* Montclair, NJ: Patterson Smith, 1969.

Wald, M.S. "Interrogations in New Haven: The Impact of Miranda." *Yale Law Journal* 76, 1966: 1521-1648.

Wallerstein, Judith S. and Joan Berlin Kelly. *Surviving the Break-Up.* New York: Basic Books, 1980.

Wax, Murray L. "On Misunderstanding *Verstehen:* a Reply to Abel." *Sociology and Social Research* 51, 1978: 323-33.

Weber, Max. *From Max Weber: Essays in Sociology,* translated by H. Gerth and C. Wright Mills. New York: Oxford University Press, 1947.

________. *Theory of Social and Economic Organization,* translated by Talcott Parsons and A.M. Henderson. Glencoe, IL: Free Press, 1947.

Weiss, W.W. and H.B. Collada. "Conciliation Counseling: The Court's Effective Mechanism for Resolving Visitation and Custody Disputes." *The Family Coordinator* 26, 1978: 444-47.

Weitzman, Lenore J. *The Divorce Revolution: The Unexpected Social and Economic Consequences for Women and Children in America.* New York: Free Press, 1985.

Wheeler, Michael. *No-Fault Divorce.* Boston: Beach Press, 1974.

Wilensky, Harold. "The Professionalization of Everyone." *American Journal of Sociology* 70, 1964: 137-58.

Whyte, William Foote. *Street-Corner Society,* 2nd ed. Chicago: University of Chicago Press, 1955.

_______. *Learning from the Field.* Beverly Hills: Sage, 1984.

Williamson, John B., David Karp, and John R. Dolphin. *The Research Craft.* Boston: Little, Brown, 1977.

Young, David M. "A Court-Mandated Workshop for Adolescent Children of Divorcing Parents: A Program Evaluation." *Adolescence* 15, Winter, 1980: 762-82.

_______. "The Divorce Experience Workshop: A Consumer Evaluation." *Journal of Divorce* 2, Fall, 1978: 37-47.

Zald, Mayer N. and Patricia Denton. "From Evangelism to General Service: The Transformation of the YWCA." *Administrative Science Quarterly* 8, no. 2, September, 1963: 214-34.

Zukerman, Jacob T. "The Family Court-Evolving Concepts." *The Annals of the American Academy of Political and Social Science,* Vol. 383, May, 1969: 119-128.

NEWSPAPERS/REPORTS

Family Court Commissioner's Office, Milwaukee County, "Statistics," 1978-83.

The Family Court of Milwaukee County. "Annual Report," 1962 & 1963.

The Family Court of Milwaukee County. "State Statutes in Wisconsin Divorce." Madison, WI, 1982.

Milwaukee Sentinel. October 6, 1967.

______. October 10, 1967.

______. March 21, 1968.

______. August 22, 1968.

______. September 30, 1969.

______. June 29, 1984.

______. April 2, 1985.

______. April 3, 1985.

______. August 15, 1985.

The Milwaukee Journal. June 9, 1976.

______. July 3, 1978.

______. August 16-20, 1982.

______. September 27, 1984.

______. November 22, 1984.

______. April 4, 1985.

SELECTED INTERVIEWS/OBSERVATIONS

Alexander, George. October 5, 1984.
Borkin, Liz. October 11, 1984.
Branden, Ellen. October 4, 1984.
Brown, Marge. March 4, 1983.
Carroll, Lawrence. September 21, 1984.
Christensen, Ted. March 2, 1983.
______. September 28, 1984.
Curley, Robert. May 15, 1984.
Davis, Russell. September 21, 1984.
______. October 12, 1984.
Foley, Leander J., Jr. September 21, 1984.
Frances, Bob. February 14, 1983.
______. June 6, 1984.
______. November 27, 1984.
Martinez, Sam. October 5, 1984.
Miller, Paul. March 3, 1984.
Murray, Don. November 1, 1984.
Phillips, Michael. February 14, 1983.
______. September 27, 1984.
Randall, Joanne. September 28, 1984.
Reilly, Robert. October 18, 1984.
Ryzek, Pat. October 12, 1984.
Samson Susan. September 21, 1984.
Schmidt, Mary. September 26, 1984.
Schwartz, Bill. March 7, 1983.
______. September 29, 1984.
______. October 4, 1984.
Steiner, Herbert. September 27, 1984.
Tucker, Betty. February 9, 1983.
______. March 1, 1983.
______. September 26, 1985.

APPENDIX A

"IN SEEKING to effect reconciliations and to safeguard the welfare of children involved in court cases affecting marriages, the family court utilizes modern marriage counseling and social services techniques. In the determination of the legal rights of the parties in divorce, legal separation, annulment, affirmation of marriage, support and maintenance of actions, it is a court of legal procedures, operating under the laws of the state. It is a partnership of these two disciplines — the law and the social approach. Like any partnership, it requires a clear allocation of roles, a clear understanding of responsibilities and a shared determination to make the partnership work." (From "The Family Court of Milwaukee County, 1962 Annual Report," p. 2.)

APPENDIX B

"DURING THE YEAR just closed, as in preceding years, the family court of Milwaukee County has had the effective cooperation of many groups. In addition to the cooperation of departments of the state, county, and city government, this working together in a common enterprise has included:

The Legal Profession. Through the Family Law Committee of the Milwaukee Bar Association, the family court has had the full cooperation of the lawyers of the community. Leaders of the local bar have consistently supported the legal-therapeutic approach to family cases, a situation not the case in many other states.

County Government. The County Executive and County Board of Supervisors have given full support to the family court, including the providing of additional clerical help to the Family Court Commissioner and Family Conciliation Department during 1963.

Community Groups. Clergymen of all religious faiths, the staff of voluntary social agencies dealing with family problems, civic organizations and interested individuals have been firm friends and full partners in the development of the family court. Milwaukee's two daily newspapers, and the radio and television media, have promoted public understanding and given full support to the family court concept.

To all who have helped, during the year 1963 and in the thirty years that have gone before, the judges, court commissioners, marriage counselors and staff members say, Thank You, for aiding in a process of development far from concluded." (From "The Family Court of Milwaukee County, 1963 Annual Report," pp. 18-19.)

APPENDIX C

FAMILY COURT COMMISSIONER STATISTICS

	1978	1979	1980	1981	1982
Actions served on FCC	6544	6228	5947	6020	5282
Motions heard by FCC	20765	20610	20365	22925	23956
Paternity motions heard	-0-	-0-	-0-	7335*	20931
Motions to vacate	7	4	10	6	3
Cases Filed with Clerk of Circuit Court:					
Divorces	5973	5569	5704	5420	4731
Legal Separations	127	125	138	120	105
Annulments	57	49	31	49	29
Affirmations of Marriage	3	3	0	4	6
Support & Maintenance, etc.	377	485	498	998	865
	6537	6231	6371	6591	5736
Cases Disposed of:					
Divorces	5114	4847	5097	5761	5317
Legal Separations	135	96	99	148	126
Annulments	45	45	48	49	36
Affirmations of Marriage	1	1	3	3	7
Support & Maintenance, etc.	60	242	155	1303	1164
	5355	5231	5402	7264	6650
Cases Dismissed	1042	596	1003	1559	1808
Reciprocal Cases Filed	675	671	765	656	502
Reciprocal Cases Disposed of	416	290	105	2086	1354
Office Contempts Commenced (Fugitive Fathers)	2244	2176	1902	1902	1594

*July thru December. Total for entire year 10,368.

APPENDIX D

767.13 Family court commissioner; appointment; powers; oaths; assistants.

(1) COUNTIES OTHER THAN MILWAUKEE. (a) Appointment. In each county, except in a county having a population of 500,000 or more, the circuit judges for the county, subject to the approval of the chief judge of the judicial administrative district, shall, by order filed in the office of the clerk of the circuit court on or before the first Monday of July of each year, appoint some reputable attorney of recognized ability and standing at the bar as the family court commissioner for the county.

(b) Powers; civil service; oath; temporary appointment; assistants. The family court commissioner, by virtue of the office and to the extent required for the performance of the duties, has the powers of a court commissioner. The family court commissioner is in addition to the maximum number of court commissioners permitted by s. 757.68. The office of the family court commissioner, or any assistant commissioner, may be placed under a county board. Before entering upon the discharge of the duties the family court commissioner shall take and file the official oath. The person appointed shall continue to act until a successor is appointed and qualified, except that in the event of disability or extended absence the judges may appoint another reputable attorney to act as temporary family court commissioner. The county board may provide that one or more assistant family court commissioners shall be appointed by the circuit judges for the county, subject to the approval of the chief judge of the judicial administrative district. An assistant family court commissioner shall have the same qualifications as the commissioner and shall take and file the official oath.

(1m) REVIEW OF THE DECISIONS OF THE FAMILY COURT COMMISSIONERS. Upon the motion of any party any decision of the family court commissioner shall be reviewed by the judge of the branch of the court to which the case has been assigned. Upon the motion of any party any such review shall include a new hearing on the subject of the decision, order or ruling.

(2) MILWAUKEE COUNTY. (a) Appointment; assistants; civil service. In counties having a population of 500,000 or more, there is created in the classified civil service the office of family court commissioner and such additional assistant family court commissioners as the county board shall determine and authorize, who shall be appointed from the membership of the bar residing in the county by the chief judge of the judicial administrative district under ss. 63.01 to 63.17.

(b) Oath; powers; salary; unavailability; duties. Before entering upon the performance of their duties, the family court commissioner and assistant family court commissioners shall take and file the official oath. The family court commissioner and assistant family court commissioners, shall, by virtue of their respective positions and to the extent required for the performance of their duties, each have the powers of a court commissioner. They shall receive such salary as may be fixed by the county board, shall perform their duties under the direction of the chief judge of the judicial administrative district or a designee and shall be furnished with quarters and necessary office furnishings and supplies. The county board shall provide them their necessary stenographic and investigational service. When the family court commissioner is unavailable, any assistant family court commissioner shall perform all the duties and have all the powers of the family court commissioner as directed by the commissioner or by the chief judge of the judicial administrative district or other judge as the chief judge may designate. In addition to the duties of the family court commissioner under this chapter, the family court commissioner shall perform other duties as the chief judge of the judicial administrative district, or other judge as the chief judge may designate, directs.

(4) RETIRED JUDGES. In any county one or more retired or former judges may be appointed as temporary or temporary assistant family court commissioners by a majority of the judges of such county. Such temporary or temporary assistant family court commissioners shall be compensated by the county.

From State Statues in Wisconsin Divorce. Madison, Wisconsin: 1982.

APPENDIX E

FAMILY COURT COMMISSIONER STATISTICS

	1979	1980	1981	1982	1983
Accounts collected thru FCC hearings:					
Reimbursement to Milw. County for welfare grants	$ 258,462	$ 186,036	$ 153,182	$ 94,273	$ 93,979
Reimbursement to Wis. Dept. of Health & Social Services for welfare grants	5,723,662	5,821,508	6,268,828	7,598,664	6,678,685
Reimbursement to Milw. County DSS and Wis. Dept. of Health & Social Services thru URESA proceedings.	16,668	14,584	5,234	3,413	3,397
Reimbursement to Milw. County for welfare grants thru Paternity proceedings	-0-	-0-	92,265**	184,603	239,877
Reimbursement to Wis. Dept. of Health & Social Services for welfare grants thru Paternity proceedings	-0-	-0-	1,294,105**	5,045,574	4,562,248
Reimbursement to Milw. County DSS and Wis. Dept. of Health & Social Services thru URESA Paternity proceedings	-0-	-0-	596**	1,818	3,982
Grand Total Collected thru FCC hearings	$ 5,998,792	$ 6,022,128	$ 7,814,210	$12,928,345	$11,582,168
Total paid thru Clerk's Office in Matrimonial and Paternity Matters	$30,705,328	$32,593,539	$38,373,690	$45,065,428	$45,581,393
9 Day Suspensions	332	284	311	227	223
Income Assignments	2,485	2,000	2,198	2,347	2,375

**July thru December. Total for entire year $2,676,340

APPENDIX F

FAMILY COURT COMMISSIONER STATISTICS

	1979	1980	1981	1982	1983
Custody Evaluations	477	456	468	337	274
Other Evaluations	83	132	192	47	29
Investigate Visitation	-0-	-0-	-0-	-0-	98
Supervision and/or Mediation of Visitation	1,052	1,066	1,291	1,086	575
Court Referrals Seen for Intake Interview	Est. 1,200	1,097	1,699	1,507	1,016
Out-of-town Inquiries	-0-	-0-	-0-	9	15
Counseling Domestic Difficulties	388	565	303	418	25
Reconciliation and Divorce Adjustment Efforts	4,643	4,968	3,620	3,574	3,575

POSTSCRIPT

WHILE THE formal part of this study was concluded in late 1985, a major structural change occurred at the court in May, 1986. Patricia Towers, Associate Director for Social Services of the Milwaukee County Department of Social Services, announced that in order to comply with the requirements of the Gramm-Rudman-Hollings deficit management act, the department would no longer fund Family Court Counseling Services. In the past several years, this department at the court had incurred large deficits. By June, 1986, the six social workers at the court and clerical personnel were assigned to other positions in the Milwaukee County civil service system.

Court personnel were not consulted about the feasibility of the elimination of Family Court Counseling Services, but neither did professionals at the court mount any strong, concerted opposition to the proposed move. Evaluations of social work performance at the court by judges and commissioners have always been mixed, certainly contributing to an absence of strong support for maintaining social workers at the court.

The immediate problem which the court faces at this time is how to obtain the services previously provided by Family Court Counseling Services. Among these are mandatory predivorce counseling and custody evaluations. The court has begun negotiations with community social service agencies which are interested in providing some of these services. In fact, several agencies are now offering predivorce counseling using both individual and group formats. A fee for the service is being assessed. Custody evaluations may in the future be handled by providers in the community (either agencies or private practitioners) with the individual's insurance hopefully covering the cost. If an individual is indigent, and a custody evaluation is ordered, the question arises as to who is responsible for the cost—is it the court which ordered the evaluation and thus ultimately Milwaukee County? This and other similar issues need to be resolved in order that the necessary work of the court can be accomplished. It remains to be seen whether or not the work of judges and commissioners will become more difficult due to the absence of social workers and their intervention with "problem" cases.

The fifty year partnership between the legal and social work professions at the court has come to an end. As a result, the court will play an even more limited role in assisting with the psychosocial problems which accompany family break-up. However, in spite of the court's more strictly legal approach toward dealing with family dissolution, the task of assisting individuals, parents, and children deal with the pain of break-up is a responsibility of individual citizens, legislators, and professionals if one of our most cherished institutions—the family—is to do well.

AUTHOR INDEX

Y

Z

SUBJECT INDEX